Libraries and Librarianship

*Sixty Years of Challenge and Change,
1945–2005*

George S. Bobinski

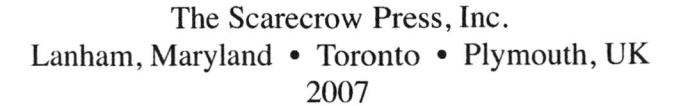

The Scarecrow Press, Inc.
Lanham, Maryland • Toronto • Plymouth, UK
2007

SCARECROW PRESS, INC.

Published in the United States of America
by Scarecrow Press, Inc.
A wholly owned subsidiary of
The Rowman & Littlefield Publishing Group, Inc.
4501 Forbes Boulevard, Suite 200, Lanham, Maryland 20706
www.scarecrowpress.com

Estover Road
Plymouth PL6 7PY
United Kingdom

British Library Cataloguing in Publication Information Available

Library of Congress Cataloging-in-Publication Data
Bobinski, George S. (George Sylvan)
  Libraries and librarianship : sixty years of challenge and change,
1945–2005 / George Bobinski.
     p. cm.
  Includes bibliographical references and index.
  ISBN-13: 978-0-8108-5899-2 (alk. paper)
  ISBN-10: 0-8108-5899-1 (alk. paper)
  1. Library science–United States–History–20th century. 2. Libraries–United
States–History–20th century. I. Title.
Z665.2.U6B62 2007
027.07309'04–dc22   2006033503

∞™ The paper used in this publication meets the minimum requirements of
American National Standard for Information Sciences—Permanence of
Paper for Printed Library Materials, ANSI/NISO Z39.48-1992.
Manufactured in the United States of America.

Dedicated to my wife, in appreciation for not only being a wonderful spouse but also a supporting professional colleague, with whom I have shared the exciting world of libraries and librarianship

Contents

Preface   ix

Acknowledgments   xi

Introduction   1

1 Changes in the Core   7

    Information Formats in Libraries   7
    The Organization of Library Information Sources   12
    Changes in Reference Service   14
    Trends in Library Management   17
    The Impact of Technology on Libraries   19

2 Types of Libraries   23

    Public Libraries   23
    The Rise of the School Library Media Center   36
    Academic Libraries   40
    Library of Congress   49
    Special Libraries   50
    The Establishment and Growth of Presidential Libraries   54
    State Library Agency Growth   55

3 Library Cooperation: Systems, Consortia, and Networks   59

4 Federal Funding, Philanthropy, and the Council on Library and Information Resources   67

Federal Aid to Libraries   67
Library Philanthropy   71
Council on Library and Information Resources   76

5 Library Associations, Intellectual Freedom, and International Relations   81

Library Professional Associations   81
Defense of Intellectual Freedom   87
International Relations   91

6 Gender and Ethnicity   95

Women in Librarianship   95
Black Librarians   97
Librarians of Other Ethnic Groups   100
Future Diversity   102

7 Library Buildings and Preservation   103

Library Buildings   103
Preservation of Library Materials   105

8 Library and Information Science Education and Library Literature   113

A Period of Growth to the Mid-1970s   114
The Closing of MLS Programs   118
Integration with Information Science   119
Changes in MLS Curriculum   120
Survival and Growth in the 1990s and at the Turn of the Century   122
Education of School Library Media Specialists   123
Tensions with Practitioners   123
Doctoral Study and Research   124
Library Literature   125

9 Prominent Leaders in the Field of Libraries
     and Librarianship   129

10 Summary and Conclusion   147

     Major Events and Developments   147
     Current Challenges   154
     Future Status of Libraries   155

Appendix: Chronology   161

Bibliography   173

Index   181

About the Author   205

Preface

The library profession is facing challenging times. The past 60 years have revolutionized our field. In order to understand the forces affecting libraries today, we need to have a clear view of the history of libraries and of communications technology.

There is value in studying library history, particularly for those attempting to make predictions about the future of libraries, but also in evaluating the present and planning for the future.

Much can be learned from the past—where we may have already dealt with similar problems as today, or where we have made mistakes that we might make again. Indeed, history can provide the foundation to understand the future.

Libraries and their 5,000 years of history have gone through constant change—sometimes revolutionary change—and so the changes that we are experiencing may not be as startling as they seem. And knowledge of the past may help us cope with the present and future. An awareness of library history will help us to adapt to change and to make the right decisions in the continuing growth and development of libraries and librarianship.

Acknowledgments

Many people helped during the time I was gathering information for this work and during the writing process. I am appreciative of the office, computer, telephone, and other resources provided to me as professor emeritus by the University at Buffalo. Special thanks to Dean David Penniman of the School of Informatics and to Dr. Judith Robinson, chair of the Department of Library and Information Studies.

The following faculty colleagues were helpful by sharing their knowledge and expertise: June Abbas, Kay Bishop, John Ellison, Melanie Kimball, Lorna Peterson, and Neil Yerkey.

Members of the University at Buffalo who provided valuable assistance include Carol Bradley, Gary Byrd, James Milles, Marcia Zubrow, and especially Cynthia Tysick.

Two graduate assistants (Jason Grubb and Ryan Phillips) tracked down elusive information, retrieved books and articles from the library or interlibrary loan, made photocopies, and so forth. Ryan Phillips typed and retyped various drafts of the manuscript and often made helpful comments. Katie Donahue, research assistant at the School of Informatics, helped in the final preparation of the manuscript.

Mary Ghikas and Judith Krug of the American Library Association provided important documents to the author.

The following other colleagues offered assistance in a variety of ways: T. Mark Hodges (Vanderbilt University); Frank G. Houdek (Southern Illinois University), and Barbara Moran (University of North Carolina at Chapel Hill).

My wife, as always, provided encouragement and support and did not mind a "retired" husband who still went to work in his office almost daily. This book is dedicated to her.

My thanks and gratitude are extended to all of the above for their assistance.

Introduction

My first job was that of a page at the Fleet branch of the Cleveland Public Library. I was not yet sixteen and had to obtain a work permit. Fleet was my neighborhood branch and I could easily walk there from home. It was early 1945 and I had for the most part grown up during World War II. I well remember when the war ended with Germany in May of 1945 and with Japan a few months later in August. I could not imagine what newspapers would write about now that the war was over. I also remember wondering what the world would be like in the future and if I would live long enough to see the next century. It seemed a long way off to a 16-year-old.

So here I am in 2006 writing about what the world has been like since 1945—particularly what the library world has been like. How libraries and librarians have changed—and how the world of information has changed!

My work as a public library page while in high school led me to a similar position in the university library at Case Western Reserve University as an undergraduate. I then went on to earn a master's degree in library science at Case Western Reserve University and later a master's in history and a PhD in library science from the University of Michigan. My MLS was followed by two years of army service during the Korean War and then by 47 years in the library profession—starting in public libraries, then in academic libraries as a college and university library director, followed by a serving as a faculty member and dean in library and information science education.

Libraries were very different in 1945 as World War II ended than they are today. There were no computers and not even copy machines. No federal funds. No public library systems or library networks. Library schools were awarding the BLS degree. Books were the overwhelming information format in library collections. The profession was certainly not diverse in terms of minority representation. Indeed, libraries in the South were segregated and few available to blacks. Men held the top library administrative positions. I have a vivid recollection of my male high school guidance counselor telling me that librarianship was a good field for men because they moved ahead rapidly in administration. I recall thinking that this seemed terribly unfair to women.

Some other dramatic differences between then and now are exemplified by the following data.

The 1948 *American Library Directory* listed 11,343 academic, public, and special libraries in the United States. Other sources showed about 14,000 school libraries in 1948 for a total of 25,334 libraries. The latest *American Library Directory* estimates 126,265 libraries (academic, public, school, and special).

The 1950 census counted 57,670 librarians (89% female). The census for 2000 showed 190,255 librarians (82% female).

In 1945, we had eleven national and regional professional associations. That number has now jumped to fifty-six.

There were 46 U.S. professional journals indexed in the *Library Literature* in 1945, while the year 2004 volume includes 160 such journals. Library science books published jumped from 66 in 1958 to 529 in the year 2003.

Library collections expanded beyond print during this period, but the print literature also increased dramatically. Books published in the United States increased from 11,022 in 1950 to 171,061 in 2003. The number of book titles in *Books in Print* jumped from 78,000 in 1948 to 1,881,192 in 2005. The number of serial titles listed in *Ulrich's Periodical Directory* rose from 7,500 in 1946 to 186,100 in 2005.

The work that follows will cover these developments and many others in greater detail, but first we must set the stage by looking at outside influences in the world around us. One cannot examine this period of library history without a look at what was going on in the United States and the world. Librarianship does not operate in a vacuum but is dependent on surrounding social, political, and economic factors. Indeed, we will see that many of the advances libraries made during this time were due to outside influences.

The appendix provides chronologies that list major events in history, in technology, and in librarianship during 1945–2005. Only some highlights are described below.

The end of the war brought normality and reconstruction—of lives as well as buildings and industry, particularly in war-ravaged countries. In the United States, the GI Bill had an immediate impact on libraries, as did the Cold War and the "Great Fear" that swept the nation during 1945–1954.

There were huge migrations of unskilled, illiterate agricultural workers from the South to the Northwest, the Midwest, and the West Coast. The extensive and purposeful investment in scientific research and technological development that began during the war grew even more in the postwar period. This would eventually lead to an information explosion.

By 1952, the television was well established as a social change agent. Korean veterans were being provided another GI Bill. The mass-market paperback was being established during this period. During the early 1950s, there was a distrust of scholars ("eggheads") and a general feeling of anti-intellectualism.

Also during the 1950s, middle-class Americans headed for the suburbs and left behind in the cities the public institutions such as libraries that their taxes had supported. At the same time, libraries were being established in the suburbs along with shopping malls. In 1954, the Supreme Court began the civil rights movement as well as the movement against segregated schools. The 1956 interstate highway act brought increasing mobility. In 1957, Sputnik created a revolution in American education.

The 1960s included many important events that had effects on library development: the assassinations of JFK and Martin Luther King; the approval of birth control pills; the War on Poverty in the Great Society programs; the influx of college students as a result of the postwar baby boom; the 1964 Civil Rights Act; the publication of Betty Friedan's *The Feminine Mystique* and the founding of the National Organization for Women (NOW); the establishment of Medicare; and the anti–Vietnam War riots.

Indeed, there was what I have called a "Golden Age of Librarianship," which progressed from the end of World War II to the early 1970s, until societal forces leveled library growth to only a slightly rising plateau during the 1970s and early 1980s.

This leveling started in 1968 with the inauguration of President Nixon. Under Nixon, the costs of the Vietnam War and the financial burden of Great Society programs led to a slackening of federal support for libraries. Also, it was the philosophy of the Nixon administration that libraries were the responsibility of state and local governments. But there were other reasons for the end of this era. School enrollments began to drop as the postwar baby boom ended and as people began to limit their family size. Higher education enrollments also slowed down. There was a growing resistance to higher taxes by taxpayers. As we moved into the 1970s, inflation became a problem.

By the 1970s, the supply of librarians was beginning to match the demand. However, the library schools were still growing and in a few years there was an oversupply of librarians and the beginning of the closure of library schools.

Since the 1970s, developments in computer and communications technology have had a major impact on libraries. This included the introduction of commercial online information services and the Apple computer in the late 1970s, the IBM personal computer and the Macintosh in the 1980s, and Microsoft's Windows, the Mosaic browser, Netscape's Navigator, and Microsoft's Internet Explorer in the 1990s. Libraries adopted the new technologies and entered a new golden age.

As the twentieth century ended with the advancement of the Internet and the World Wide Web, libraries were facing perhaps the greatest challenges in their 5,000-year history. Among these was a shift from paper to digital form as a major information medium. Another was the shift from building library collections to gaining access to information for users from wherever this information was located. The library was still a storehouse but now also served as an intermediary in the gateway to information access.

At the same time, books were being produced in increasing numbers and new library buildings were being built. And library usage and circulation statistics have been rising.

My coverage of library developments since World War II is provided through ten chapters beginning with a historical review in chapter 1 of what I call the "core of librarianship," consisting of the information formats available in or through libraries, the organization of library information sources, changes in reference service, trends in library management, and the all-embracing impact of technology on libraries.

Chapter 2 focuses on the various types of libraries. This includes historical overviews of public, school, special, and academic libraries, as well as the Library of Congress, presidential libraries, and state library agencies.

The spread of library cooperation through library systems, consortia, and networks and their impact since World War II is the topic of chapter 3.

Chapter 4 covers three distinct but related topics: federal funding, library philanthropy, and the important role of the Council on Library and Information Resources since its establishment in 1956.

Then, chapter 5 traces the growth and activities of professional library associations, the development and important roles of the concepts and practice of intellectual freedom and professional involvement in international relations with our library colleagues throughout the world.

A historical look at the role of gender and ethnicity is the focus of chapter 6.

Chapter 7 is about library buildings and about the conservation and preservation of library materials in these buildings. We look back historically on the great number of library buildings constructed during the past 60 years and at the changes in the architectural styles and interior design. We also trace the growing concern and actions to preserve our collections from disintegration and other causes of deterioration.

The dramatic change in library and information science education is the focus of chapter 8, along with a look at the growth of library literature.

A listing and description of the eminent persons who have had the greatest impact on the field during this period is provided in chapter 9.

Finally, the concluding chapter summarizes what I consider to be the major events and developments in our profession since World War II, examines the current challenges facing us, and provides some insights about the future of libraries.

An appendix includes chronologies of major events in general history, technology, and the library profession during the past 60 years.

A bibliography with some commentary is also provided, as well as acknowledgments to all who helped in the study.

The emphasis of this book is on libraries and librarianship, though there is some coverage of related activities in information science, particularly in the review of special libraries and information centers and of library and information science education. There is also some overlap and repetition of certain topics in a few chapters because of the close relationship in many different areas of the field.

I have learned a great deal during the research and writing of this study. Even though I worked professionally during most of this time span, I was not fully aware of some of the events and developments that were happening around me. As I look back now, it is evident that our profession has changed dramatically during the past 60 years. Hopefully, this work provides a record and an analysis of the changes and challenges during this period and some guidance for the future.

CHAPTER 1

Changes in the Core

This chapter covers the major developments in the traditional core areas of librarianship: information resources of libraries and how they got there, how these sources are classified and cataloged, how librarians provided assistance to their successful use, and how all of this is managed and administered. One more core area that has had an impact on everything in libraries is added at the very end: information technology. This is covered where appropriate in the four traditional areas, but an overview is provided in the last section of this chapter.

INFORMATION FORMATS IN LIBRARIES

This past 60 years have been characterized by an information explosion in two ways: a tremendous increase in the amount of material published in print and an explosion of new information medium formats. Librarians and libraries had to cope with this information explosion in their acquisitions and collection management policies. By the 1990s, they were challenged to provide access to information formats located outside the library through electronic means. First, let us deal with books.

Marshall McLuhan prophesized in 1960 that "the book is dead." He said it was too static, too linear, and too boring to compete with the newer electronic media such as television. McLuhan predicted that sometime before the turn of the century, the last physical book would be published in America, leaving nothing but electronic resources. Today's book publishing industry is alive and well, and the book remains an important media format in our libraries. Tables 1.1 and 1.2 show some supporting historical data.

Table 1.1.   Books Published in the United States

Year	No. of Books
1950	11,022
1960	15,012
1970	36,071
1980	43,377
1990	46,743
2000	122,108*
2003	171,061

*In 1997, a count of 67,796 was upgraded because of un-
dercounting. Up to this point, only the books catalogued
by the Library of Congress had been counted. Not included were inexpensive editions, annuals, and many
small publishers and self-published books. (Also, the U.S.
imported 851,850,000 volumes from other countries during this year.)

Table 1.2.   Number of Books in Print

Year	No. of Books
1948	78,000
1990	850,012
2005	1,881,192

The increase in book productivity, which is worldwide, is due not only to demand but also to advances in modern technology. Digitized text and fast laser printing have made it possible for publishers to print even one additional copy of already published books on demand or small runs of new books. Declining prices for digitally controlled, high-speed laser printers have changed the economics of a business that had been ruled by high-volume production, making it possible to publish highly specialized books that would not have been published otherwise.

Serials show a similar growth. In 1947, *Ulrich's Periodicals Directory* listed some 7,500 serials. The 2005 Ulrich's database shows 186,100 active serials (including over 700 titles in library and information science). *Ulrich* also now includes active online journals, which are continuing to increase, as shown in table 1.3.

It is interesting to examine the book and serial holding of OCLC's WorldCat in comparison to nonprint holdings (see table 1.4). This is a union catalog of more than 9,000 OCLC members in 80 countries with bibliographic records spanning four millennia of recorded knowledge

Table 1.3.   **Number of Active Online Serials in the United States**

Year	No. of Active Online Serials
2001	20,430
2003	34,500
2005	39,000

Table 1.4.   **OCLC WorldCat Listings as of July 2005**

Medium	Number	Percentage
Books	48,763,726	84.12%
Serials	2,681,614	4.63%
Visual Materials	1,889,084	3.26%
Maps	866,548	1.49%
Mixed Materials	255,941	0.44%
Sound Recordings	1,983,295	3.42%
Scores	1,293,931	2.23%
Computer Files	234,649	0.40%
Total	57,968,788	100%

in every form of human experience, from stone tablets to websites, in more than 400 languages.

Nonbook materials also had an explosive growth after World War II. As the war ended, library holdings were overwhelmingly book and serial oriented. But there were some collections of maps, music, newspapers, scores, pamphlets, phonorecords, photographs, and film, as well as government documents, manuscripts, and archival holdings in some libraries.

In 1948, the Carnegie Corporation funded public library film circuits in Cleveland and at the Missouri State Library. It also funded the establishment of the Film Advisory Service at the American Library Association to promote public libraries as distribution centers for film and other audiovisual materials.

During the 1950s and 1960s, film libraries and collections expanded because of increasing government aid to education. This occurred not only in public libraries but also in school libraries and in libraries serving higher education.

Following World War II, the use of microform became common among libraries. These included microfilm, microcard, and microfiche. They made out-of-print or specialized material such as theses available.

They also saved space, increased access, and preserved fragile items but required special viewing equipment and copy service.

There were many other information formats that appeared in library collections in the postwar period. Among these were filmstrips, multimedia kits, slides, realia, audio books, and sculpture and art reproductions. Some public libraries even loaned umbrellas and tools!

Existing media formats went through a number of transformations. The phonograph disc went from 78 RPM to 33-1/3 RPM and 45 RPM to long playing, to reel-to-reel tape, to cassette, to CD, and to DVD. Film evolved to videotape, videodisc, VCR, and DVD.

In the late 1970s, libraries began to experiment with videodiscs. These were multimedia presentations of information on laser disks, including media formats such as text, video clips, sound recordings, maps, and so forth that matured in the 1980s and eventually evolved into CDs and DVDs.

In the 1980s, CD-ROM technology provided libraries with multimedia resources that contained encyclopedias, information banks or numeric data, bibliographies, electronic retrieval databases, and even full-text access.

During the 1980s, the advent of the videocassette recorder/player (VCR) permitted libraries of all types to acquire (at a reasonable cost), store, and circulate videos in convenient, easy-to-use formats with minimal potential for damage. For public libraries in particular, this became a popular item that helped boost circulation figures. VCRs are now being replaced by DVDs. Audiobooks also grew in quantity and popularity among library users.

As we entered the 1990s, revolutionary developments occurred in information access with the growth of the Internet and the World Wide Web. Libraries were not only building collections within their locations but also providing access to collections and information sources in other locations. Indeed, the emphasis was now on access rather than ownership. They also began to develop digital collections from a wide variety of sources, including

- the library's own holdings that had been digitized
- purchased datasets on CD-ROM
- purchased datasets that were online

- electronic publications that had a paper equivalent
- electronic publications that had no paper equivalent
- electronic reference works, which increasingly had no paper equivalent
- e-books

Electronic books—also called e-books—were also developed at this time. Many different types became available; some were designed to be distributed electronically but printed out for reading. Others were intended to be read on a computer or on a specially designed e-book reader. Electronic journals, both scholarly and popular, became increasingly available.

Indeed, by 2005 through OCLC's NetLibrary, libraries could gain access to the e-content of over 90,000 titles of e-books, audiobooks, and e-journals. And this number was growing. Library users could access NetLibrary content wherever they were—library, home, or office.

In late 2004, Google announced that it was embarking on an ambitious project to digitally scan selected books from the collections of five major research libraries and make them available online. The libraries involved are Harvard, Stanford, Oxford, the University of Michigan, and the New York Public Library.

The latest data from the National Center for Educational Statistics shows the impact of information formats on library collections. Shown in table 1.5 are total expenditures on acquisitions for the year 2002–2003.

Table 1.5.   Library Acquisition Expenditures in 2002–2003

Medium	Academic Libraries	Public Libraries
Books	$ 267,260,940	$391,061,507
Other Print	15,315,122	9,838,842
Serials	512,076,817	57,544,387
Manuscript and Archives	1,766,000	423,124
Audiovisual Equipment	6,650,270	20,372,849
Audiovisual Materials	4,199,411	38,224,921
Microform	27,953,850	7,694,797
Electronic Reference	91,630,622	49,997,553
Preservation	15,846,402	2,526,300
Total	$1,352,674,991	$950,577,068

THE ORGANIZATION OF LIBRARY INFORMATION SOURCES

With the growth of libraries and collections, there was an increase in the number of and demand for catalogers for almost three decades after 1945. Most libraries had many catalogers trying to keep up with increasing materials being added to their collections, which resulted in a lot of redundant original cataloging being done in thousands of libraries.

Two important cataloging tools were published in 1949: *A.L.A. Cataloguing Rules for Authors and Title Entries* and a companion volume entitled *Rules for Descriptive Cataloguing in the Library of Congress.*

Then, in 1967, four events occurred that made that time a banner year in the cataloging revolution. First, there was the development of MARC. Director Quincy Mumford and Henriette Avram at the Library of Congress provided a standardized format for a machine-readable catalog (MARC) record for all digital bibliographic records. A common language was incorporated in online catalogs. This sparked a commitment to standardization, communication, and cooperation among libraries.

Second was the establishment of OCLC in 1967 at the Ohio College Library Center. Fred Kilgour began OCLC with a vision of linking all libraries through a common database. Within a few years, there were no longer hordes of individual catalogers in each library duplicating the work of others or doing cataloging that was not standardized.

Third was the introduction of the Standard Book Number (ISBN) for each published book. This was followed by the adoption of ISSN for serial publications.

And fourth was the publication of *The Anglo-American Cataloging Rules*—which was completed in two versions, a North American text and a British text—which helped to advance cooperation by encouraging the spread of shared cataloging.

On another more traditional note, in 1968 the Library of Congress began publishing the *National Union Catalog of Pre-1956 Imprints,* which totaled 754 volumes when completed in 1981—just as online catalogs were being established. When completed by Mansell Publishers, the project cost over $34 million, contained 528,000 pages of text, and consumed 130 linear feet of shelving.

In 1971, Cataloging in Publication (CIP) was introduced by the Library of Congress. Also in 1971, the OCLC shared cataloging system was made available online in the state of Ohio. In 1978, it was made available as a national system.

During 1978, the second edition of *The Anglo-American Cataloging Rules* (AACR2) was published. This brought uniformity to cataloging practice in the English-speaking world and became an almost worldwide code.

In 1979, Stanford University joined the Research Libraries Group, and its BALLOTS network was renamed the Research Library Information Network (RLIN) and began to offer services similar to OCLC but aimed at the large research libraries.

The machine-readable catalog records mentioned above were first used to produce book catalogs and then computer-output microfilm catalogs. A few libraries developed quite sophisticated online catalogs during the mid to late 1970s, but the early 1980s saw a burst of activity with online public access catalogs (OPACS) and the retirement of the venerable card catalog.

In 1991, OCLC launched PRISM, which offered enhanced capabilities for online cataloging and searching online catalogs. By 2002, using OCLC's WorldCat, a cataloger could search the database for bibliographic records for items being cataloged and would be certain to find such records about 95% of the time. If no record was found, the cataloger could create a new record and input it into WorldCat—making it possible for only one library to create an original catalog record for an item and then provide a means for other libraries to use the same new record for their catalogs. Indeed, WorldCat made it possible for libraries to not only catalog items but also to select and obtain materials ready for shelving.

Some three decades ago, every single library was responsible for cataloging its own material. Even though the Library of Congress printed and sold catalog cards, each library upon receipt of a new book was responsible for verifying the author and title, assigning subject headings and a classification number, and printing and filing cards in the library's error-ridden card catalog, all at great cost. This all changed in the 1970s.

In summary, then, MARC was accepted and used throughout the world and became the basis for almost all automated bibliographic systems. By the turn of the millennium, together with AACR2 and ISBN,

MARC provided a universally accepted standard for recording descriptive data and almost a universal cataloging code for traditional and electronic material.

CHANGES IN REFERENCE SERVICE

There was an expansion of reference service in libraries in the post–World War II period for a variety of reasons. Many new libraries were established while others expanded their buildings and services. With the explosion of knowledge and publications, library users needed more assistance. There was also an increase in the number of reference users as the baby boom hit schools and institutions of higher education.

In the late 1940s and 1950s, public libraries expanded telephone reference services. In the larger libraries, special desks and even rooms with quick-reference collections were established for this service.

There was an increase in subject departments in medium and large public libraries in the 1950s and 1960s, with reference staff provided in each area. The same occurred in large academic libraries as collections grew and were dispersed among locations. Some university libraries began to establish undergraduate libraries with individualized reference service.

With the great influx of students in the 1960s, academic libraries began to offer bibliographic instruction on a larger scale (more on this in the upcoming section on academic libraries).

Another reference service developed in the 1960s was the establishment of Information and Referral centers (I&R). Found most often in urban libraries, they drew upon unconventional resources and emphasized practical information relating to basic human needs for food, clothing, shelter, employment, and health services. They strove to work closely with governmental, social, and community agencies.

The 1960s and 1970s saw the spread of public library systems and multitype library systems. These began to provide advanced and specialized reference service to member libraries and their users. The nine regional reference and research councils organized in New York State are a prime example of this.

But the greatest change in reference service came about from the advances in computer and communication technology.

In 1945, Vannevar Bush proposed using electronics and light to search a compact storage medium. His imaginary MEMEX machine used keyboards and levers to punch in an index code that would retrieve and display prerecorded documents. MEMEX would also include built-in aids to the process of thinking and memory. This was certainly a prophetic proposal!

We have seen that the years following WWII experienced a huge growth in the volume of scholarly literature. Traditional print methods of gathering and searching for information were breaking down. People began to see the computational, storage, and searching possibilities of computers as possible solutions for controlling the explosion of new bibliographic information.

In the early 1960s, indexing and abstracting services began using computers to automate their production process by storing and connecting bibliographic information to machine-readable magnetic tape. The National Library of Medicine started storing information from its *Index Medicus* print index to tape, which became the basis for the MEDLINE system. Storing information on magnetic tapes could not provide random access but rather clumsy and time-consuming batch searching on an enormous mainframe computer.

During the 1970s, computer databases began to reach a wider audience. New hard-drive storage systems greatly increased the power, memory, and performance of computers and permitted random access to data and multiple simultaneous users. The establishment of new national and international communications networks made it possible to remotely access bibliographic databases.

In 1972, Lockheed Company made its DIALOG service available and ORBIT, BRS, LexisNexis, and others were soon to follow. Libraries were among the first subscribers to the new online services in the mid-1970s as vast stores of bibliographic information could now be accessed and efficiently processed. However, access to online information required the use of trained intermediaries—online searchers—who quickly assumed a prominent role in libraries during the late 1970s and early 1980s. Indeed, by 1980, electronic reference emerged as distinct from the print-oriented reference desk. A patron wishing to do an online literature search had to work through a librarian trained in online searching.

Then another dramatic change occurred. CD-ROM technology began to enter libraries in the mid-1980s and continued to dominate into the mid-1990s. Compact disk read-only memory became possible to use because of the appearance of IBM's microcomputer in 1981. About the same time, Phillips and Sony created the first audio disc in 1982 for storing music. In 1983, they released a data-bearing disk that could be used with microcomputers. A massive storage capacity made CD-ROM an attractive medium to house data of all types.

CD-ROM technology found rapid acceptance in libraries. Within a short time, there were CD-ROM bibliographic databases and nonbibliographic material such as dictionaries, encyclopedias, directories, and other standard reference sources. CD-ROM library technology allowed patrons to access computer databases on their own without incurring telecommunications or database charges of using an online system. By the early 1990s, there was a large end-user community using CD-ROM technology providing wide access to electronic resources. Online searching began serving a diminishing base of patrons.

In 1991, OCLC's FirstSearch was launched as the first end-user reference system in the library community. It was designed to be used by both librarians and library patrons, a departure from the bibliographic databases. Initially it started small, with WorldCat and five databases. FirstSearch is now an online search tool that delivers content from WorldCat and dozens of databases of bibliographic and full-text content.

Beginning in the early 1990s, a new technology linked computers together in a vast supernetwork known as the Internet, which allowed librarians to retrieve a mass of electronic information from computers around the world. The Internet was enhanced by the development of the World Wide Web (WWW), a multimedia hyperlinked interface that could access information across the entire Internet. The WWW really became a practical possibility with the appearance of the Mosaic browser in 1993, which evolved into the Netscape's Navigator and Microsoft's Internet Explorer, which in turn brought the WWW to the general public. After 1995, the WWW became the dominant interface for getting information over the Internet.

Libraries quickly took advantage of the Internet's potential. Such applications as e-mail, WWW, and listservs were rapidly integrated into library operations by the end of the 1990s. The WWW was used as platforms to present locally important electronic resources. Library cata-logs, CD-ROM resources, online databases, and open Internet access were often integrated into gateways that permitted libraries to offer electronic sources and services more efficiently.

The Internet revolutionized reference work. Reference transactions could now take place outside the walls of the library. E-mail made it possible for people to use library services from their home or work-place twenty-four hours, seven days a week. Reference librarians could not only interact with patrons on the Internet but also extend their search for needed information anywhere in the world.

Library patrons began using the Internet to tap into a vast array of electronic information, and traditional requests at the reference desk began to decline. Reference librarians began spending more time in-structing patrons in the use of information technology and less time try-ing to track down specific pieces of information. Helping patrons to ask better questions, evaluate information, and understand information structures—in short, teaching information literacy skills—became an important role of reference librarians.

The Internet had an effect on both online searching and CD-ROMs in libraries. Online searching (primarily Web-based) was still an option but in decline. The role of the CD-ROM was also diminished. Bibliographic databases were increasingly delivered through Internet-based platforms and fewer appeared in CD-ROM format. Electronic reference service had its origins just thirty years ago. And within the 1990s, reference li-brarians went from intermediary online to CD-ROM to Web systems.

Librarians continue to find answers to questions or help library users do so. The latest NCES data (2003) shows that public libraries an-swered more than 305 million reference questions. Older available data from 2000 reported 75 million reference questions were answered in academic libraries. By the year 2004, 99 percent of academic libraries and large- and medium-sized public libraries offered digital reference services through e-mail on the Web.

TRENDS IN LIBRARY MANAGEMENT

Specific developments in academic, public, school, and special library management will be discussed in the appropriate sections of this study, but there are some general library management trends since World War II that need to be mentioned. Among these are the following:

- During the late 1940s and the 1950s, library administrators generally remained unacquainted with management principles. Planning and organization to achieve specific objectives was not commonly practiced in libraries.
- The growth in collective bargaining and unionization became particularly strong beginning in the 1960s.
- The democratization of library management style made its appearance. Participative library management had its origins in the late 1960s and continued into the 1970s and 1980s.
- The entry of many more women into top library administrative positions began in the 1970s and continues today.

More recent trends that started in the 1990s have included the following:

- The changing organization of libraries. Most have become more decentralized and less hierarchical. Staff teams have been implemented in many of them.
- A change in the composition of people who work in libraries. There have been growing proportions of paraprofessionals and professional librarians who have been doing more actual management work. There has also been a growing number of specialized departments such as systems, public relations, and fund-raising. The acceptance of other kinds of degrees in addition to the MLS degree has become more common.
- The growing importance of fund-raising. Libraries have had to become less dependent on government funding and more on grants, gifts, and self-generated income.
- Increasing importance of planning in libraries of all types—especially strategic planning.
- Greater emphasis on staff development and lifelong learning as libraries continue to change.
- Increase in stress and burnout produced by a rapidly changing environment, tight budgets, and sometimes by demanding patrons.

Another trend that began in the 1990s was an increase in outsourcing and privatization of certain library operations and even entire libraries. At the 2001 annual conference, the ALA Council adopted a policy stating "the American Library Association opposes the shifting of policy making and management of library services from the public to the private sector."

The latest government data on the library work force is from 2001–2003 sources and is shown in table 1.6.

Table 1.6. Library Personnel, 2002–2003

Type of Library	Librarians	Other Paid Staff	Total Staff
Academic libraries	25,152	70,291	95,433
Public libraries	44,920	91,300	136,220
School libraries	66,471	99,557	166,028
State libraries	1,201	2,631	3,832
Total	137,744	263,779	401,523

Comparable figures for employment in special libraries (e.g., libraries serving businesses, scientific agencies, hospital, law firms, and nonprofit organizations) are not available.

In 2004, some 26 percent of librarians were union members, while an additional 30 percent were represented by unions.

Finally, the advent of the Internet, the World Wide Web, and e-mail have all affected many library management operations, particularly in communicating with staff and users.

THE IMPACT OF TECHNOLOGY ON LIBRARIES

We have already touched on many of the impacts of technology on libraries in the preceding sections of this chapter. This section brings these together and provides a wider perspective of this important force. The advent of the computer and its applications to librarians—automation, databases, online resources, the Internet, the World Wide Web, and e-mail—all changed the way libraries use and share information. Libraries were revolutionized, resulting in resource sharing, development of consortia, and the onset of online catalogs. By the mid-1990s, there was a dramatic shift in focus from ownership to access. Libraries were no longer only warehouses of information in all media formats but also conduits for information—wherever it might be.

There have been two aspects to the impact of computers on libraries. First, there was library automation. This involved the use of computers to make circulation, cataloging, serials control, and online searching much more efficient. The second was library digitization. This made some of the information content of libraries available in digitized form, stored, and made accessible in computer systems.

But let us begin the historical review even before the advent of the computer. In 1945, there were no copy machines or computers in libraries. In the late 1940s, one could see announcements in the professional journals about microcards, library punch-card procedures, and a photocharger becoming available. The 1940s and 1950s brought the advent of microform storage of information. Thermofax photocopying was announced in the 1950s. The Xerox copier became available in 1959.

A major showcase for futuristic library technology was ALA's Library-21 exhibit at the Seattle World's Fair in 1962. Its aim was to show what an electronic information center would be like in the year 2000. There was a UNIVAC Solid State 90 computer with an attached printer surrounded by public work desks. Three kinds of information sources could be queried: a personalized bibliography from records of about 8,000 books; a data bank containing quotations of 74 authors from the Great Books of the Western World series; and a gazetteer of information on 92 nations. The planning committee for the exhibit also made a proposal for a computerized national information network that might be brought online within 10 years!

One of the most influential and stimulating works on the potential of computer technology in libraries was J. C. R. Licklider's *Libraries of the Future,* published in 1965 by MIT Press. This study, commissioned by the Council on Library Resources (CLR), was led by Dr. Licklider of MIT along with a team of engineers and psychologists. They foresaw networks and the Web, and the work was enthusiastically embraced by library leaders. It was also an early example of the importance of CLR.

Automation fever began to sweep libraries in the 1960s. Indeed, there were many optimistic forecasts of automation in the mid-1960s. There were comic disasters that befell pioneering efforts to adapt computers to libraries at this time. Some careers were damaged and library administrations collapsed—but out of these failures and trial and error came success. We have already read about the development of the MARC record and the establishment of the Ohio College Library Centers in 1967.

The 1970s, as stated above, saw the development of the large commercial databases such as DIALOG and BRS, which became available to academic institutions, libraries, industry, and individuals. Librarians began to serve as mediators for their clients in online searching. Minicomputers were also developed and made available at this time.

Still another 1970s occurrence was networking, with the linking of computers followed by the growth of multitype library cooperation. OCLC and other bibliographic utilities allowed libraries to work cooperatively across political and type of library lines. There was now the quick ability to see what libraries around the world owned, which improved interlibrary loan immensely. We stopped being just collections in a library building and became a world of information—a library without walls. The venerable card catalog became an online catalog.

Library automation continued to become widespread. Single-function systems, using computers to manage circulation, acquisitions, serial control, and cataloging, gave way in the 1980s to integrated systems using a single bibliographic database to support multiple library operations, including public access catalogs (OPACS).

The 1980s also brought further technology advances. The advent of the personal computer changed the lives of most people and of libraries. Facsimile transmission, desktop publishing, artificial intelligence, and the development of CD-ROM all had important impacts. CD-ROM provided a database on a disk, which permitted libraries to offer access to the page files of machine-readable information without telecommunication cost or fear of destruction of information. But, of course, updates also had to be provided.

The 1990s saw the availability of the Internet, the World Wide Web, and e-mail. The development of the Web browser and billions of Web pages monumentally changed the way we publish, communicate, and access information. The whole concept of remote access to information from the Web began to revolutionize library services. The Internet, Web, and e-mail have also changed the way our patrons look for information.

The latest technological developments have included library adoptions of blogging and podcasting. The weblog, an online journal listed in reverse chronological order with the most recent post on top, is beginning to be used by libraries—especially public libraries—as a library news page, for staff discussion, announcing acquisitions and services, book club discussion, and promoting children's and adult programs.

Since late 2001, over 30 million people have purchased iPod/MP3 players, portable and lightweight digital audio players, and are listening to audio content relevant to their interests without having a radio or computer. This includes music collections, radio content, or their own recorded audio. Podcast directory sites have emerged to help listeners locate new podcasts.

Libraries have begun to use this new technology. The South Huntington (New York) Library was one of the first public libraries to circulate iPods. The Baylor University Fine Arts Library began circulating 12 iPods loaded with course reserves for music classes. The Newport Beach (California) Public Library loaded audiobooks on iPod Shuffles and lent them to patrons.

The following description of the Cuneiform Digital Library Initiative is dramatic evidence of the merging of the old and new in librarianship. Library collections have their origins with clay tablets in Mesopotamia almost 5,000 years ago. Over time, these collections were lost or scattered throughout the world. These cuneiform or wedge-shaped tablets hold the written record of how people lived, labored, and ruled at that time, including such information as creation myths, legal codes, medical prescriptions, and business ledgers. Since 1998, historians using the modern language of computers are assembling a virtual library of these earliest known written documents as part of the Cuneiform Digital Library Initiative. About 120,000 tablets are being identified all over the world. The goal is to catalog, photograph, and post each one on the Web. A Web-based dictionary of Sumerian, the first written language, is also being completed.

In closing, one can say that throughout this period libraries used a variety of techniques and technologies to acquire, give access to, disseminate, and preserve recorded information. How they did this depended on the needs of their users and the type of library. We explore these aspects in forthcoming pages.

CHAPTER 2

Types of Libraries

This chapter provides a historical review of the different types of libraries—public, school, academic, and special—as well as a brief overview of the Library of Congress, the presidential libraries, and state libraries. The Library of Congress is included here because of its importance as a "de facto" national library, the presidential libraries are shown as an example of new libraries and information centers formed after World War II, and the state libraries have a key role in library development in most states.

PUBLIC LIBRARIES

The number of public libraries grew from 7,172 in 1948 to 9,734 (plus 7,237 branches) in 2004; in addition, most were in new or enlarged buildings with expanded collections in all media formats and members of a public library system.

And yet the core of public library service had already been available in the immediate postwar period. Through their collections of books, public libraries attempted to meet the informational, educational, and recreational needs of a clientele ranging from age two to 82 and up, including students in kindergarten and those seeking their PhDs. Most public libraries at that time provided specialized services to children, many to adults, and a smaller number to young adults. Reading was promoted by reading lists, exhibits, programs, and reader's advisory service. Reference service was also available; indeed, the large public libraries had subject divisions with specialized reference services.

This historical overview of public library development in the United States since World War II is presented through the following topics: social impact, federal aid and financial support, technology, standards and planning documents, collection development, adult services, children and young adult services, and a look at public libraries today.

Social Impact

Beginning in the 1950s and into the 1960s, changes in class and ethnic mixes had an impact on urban public libraries. They lost many of their regular users to the growing suburbs, which themselves established and/or enlarged school and public libraries. Left behind were the educationally disadvantaged and poor white, black, and foreign-born residents. Downtowns became deserted at night, and downtown stores followed the middle-class residents to the suburbs. The tax base eroded and the political power shifted to the suburbs. Central libraries with large and specialized collections remained in downtown areas and their resources could not be readily duplicated in the suburbs. These central libraries and the urban branch libraries now had different clientele with different needs.

Throughout much of the South, almost all public libraries were segregated and those serving blacks were fewer in number and with much less financial support. By the 1960s, these social barriers began to fall and black citizens began to have access to all public libraries.

In the 1990s, new migrations had an affect on public libraries. These national migrations were from East to West from North to South, from the Snow Belt and Rust Belt to the Sun Belt and the Pacific Northwest. Population growth in these areas brought new investments, new jobs, and expanded and/or new public libraries.

The 1990s also brought new immigration from Asia and Latin America, placing new demands on public libraries. Public libraries also tried to deal with the homeless and those who had no access to all the new information technology. The senior citizen population also grew in great numbers.

But away from the urban areas, the vast majority of public libraries throughout the country were small and scattered among smaller communities. In the year 2002, 30% of all libraries had operating expenditures of less than $50,000 per year while 41% had operating costs of $50,000–$399,999. The one difference was that in the late 1940s these small public libraries stood alone; by the 1970s and 1980s, however, they were probably members of a public library system with access to wider resources.

Federal Aid and Financing

Federal aid to libraries is covered elsewhere, but at least a brief mention of it needs to be made here since the major thrust of financial support for public libraries came after the end of World War II. The American Library Association (ALA) made a decision through its Washington office to focus requests for federal aid on rural services to reach those previously unserved by urban libraries. Success was achieved in 1956 with the Library Services Act (LSA). Funding was provided to states for library service to areas with less than 10,000 people. State library agencies had to submit plans to the U.S. Office of Education.

The LSA extended library service to more than 40,000,000 people and was renewed in 1960. In 1964, the 10,000-population limit was removed and construction money was now also available—just at the right time as the Carnegie libraries, built earlier in the century, needed expansion or replacement. The Library Services and Construction Act (LSCA) of 1964 continued to strengthen state library agencies and encourage interlibrary cooperation just as the concept of public library systems was spreading.

President Nixon favored zero federal funding for libraries but was fortunately overruled by Congress. The same was true for President Reagan and into the 1990s.

Local financial support was excellent when public libraries had their great growth from the late 1940s through the early 1970s. In the 1970s, double-digit inflation, the Vietnam War, and an energy crisis brought disaster budgets for public libraries—as well as a tax revolt and a conservative, antigovernment atmosphere. There were some years of better times, but then an ideological trend to reduce government expenditures and taxes—though directed against welfare bureaucracy—spilled over to the curtailment of support for public education, libraries, and the arts.

At the same time, public libraries were facing the rising costs of books and of adding new media formats and electronic resources as well as services for new population groups. According to the University of Illinois Library Research Center, the public library expenditures index went up from 81 in 1993 to 109 in 2003 (in the year 2000 dollars). This may appear impressive but inflation took up much of the gain.

Technology

Like other types of libraries, public libraries were also greatly affected by new technology—particularly in the 1980s and 1990s. It began with automatic scanners attached to automated circulation files. Along with mechanized circulation came new control measures for preventing theft. Databases accessed by computers and computerized catalogs followed. The public library became an access point on the information highway—especially for those who had no access to their own computers. In 2002, 98.7% of public libraries had access to the Internet.

By 2005, public libraries were continuing to adopt the new technologies as seen in these two examples. The New York Public Library launched its Audio Program, making more than 700 popular, educational, and literary titles available for downloading through the library's website. The Denver Public Library became the first public library to offer downloadable video and film to its patrons.

Standards and Planning Documents

The period from 1945 through the mid-1980s was an amazing one in terms of public library standards and planning documents.

The *Post War Standards for Public Libraries* (1943) provided qualitative and quantitative standards and a brief primer on public library administration. They stated that over 35 million Americans lacked any kind of public library service, that most public libraries were too small to be able to provide adequate service, and that financial support for public libraries was far too low.

The *National Plan for Public Library Service* (1948) identified 50 million people in the United States who were well served by public libraries, 50 million who were poorly served, and 35 million who had no public library service. The plan proposed a drastic restructuring of public libraries, reducing the number of smaller libraries. Also recommended were stronger state library agencies, statewide planning, certification of librarians, increased state aid, and federal aid.

Very important in public library development was the Public Library Inquiry, funded by the Carnegie Corporation in the late 1940s, which resulted in nineteen special studies undertaken by the Social Science Research Council in response to the ALA's request for an appraisal in sociological, cultural, and human terms of the public libraries' actual and potential contribution to American society. The inquiry was very influential in the reformulation of standards, in the continuing development and implementation of standards, in the continuing development and implementation of the concept of larger units of service, and in the eventual achievement of federal aid to public libraries beginning in 1956.

The *Public Library Service: A Guide to Evaluation* appeared in 1956. These ALA standards represented an official endorsement of the new approach to library organization and service. Libraries working together, by sharing their services and materials, could meet the full needs of their users. This cooperative approach on the part of libraries was the single most important recommendation of this document. In addition, the standards made clear that the new systems were not meant to threaten the local public library: "The development of systems of libraries does not weaken or eliminate the small community library. On the contrary, it offers that library and its users greatly expanded resources and services."

Standards for Work with Young Adults followed in 1959. There were also *Standards for Children's Services in Public Libraries*, which was issued in 1964. Another specialized set of standards was *Guidelines for Audiovisual Materials and Services for Public Libraries* (1970).

In 1967, *Minimum Standards for Public Library Systems, 1966* was published by ALA. The title change certainly emphasized the shift in approach from single libraries to cooperative systems. The 1967 document introduced a hierarchy of library service consisting of the community library, the system headquarters, and the state library agency.

The above publications proposed standards that public libraries were urged to achieve. Beginning in 1979, the emphasis was on how to evaluate public library service and how to plan for its future. First came the *Public Library Mission Statement* in 1979, which focused attention on goals and objectives. It asserted that a single national set of standards was not appropriate.

Next (1980), the *Planning Process for Public Libraries* promoted planning within each library in order to establish goals and programs suited to the local community. The document prescribed seven steps for the planning process:

1. Assessing community library needs.
2. Evaluating current library services and resources.
3. Determining the role of the public library in the community.
4. Setting goals, objectives, and priorities.
5. Developing and evaluating strategies for change.
6. Implementing strategies.
7. Monitoring and evaluating progress towards goals and objectives.

Within each library, this sequence was to be directed and coordinated by a planning committee composed of staff, trustees, and community members. Several factors were stressed: the importance of gathering data about the community and the library, the need for establishing goals and priorities, the evaluation of performance, and willingness to consider change. The process was to be thought of as ongoing rather than as a one-shot exercise.

Two other important publications during this time were *Output Measures for Public Libraries* (1982) and *Cost Funding for Public Libraries* (1985). In 1987, a second edition of *Output Measures* was published.

In *Planning and Role Setting for Public Libraries* (1987), with data in hand about both the community and the library, the planners were to select among possible roles for the public library, accepting some and rejecting others, and then setting priorities among those that were accepted. The eight roles suggested were:

1. Community activities center: The library is a central focus point for community activities, meetings, and services.
2. Community information center: The library is a clearinghouse for current information on community organizations, issues, and services.

3. Formal education support center: The library assists students of all ages in meeting educational objectives established during their formal courses of study.
4. Independent learning center: The library supports individuals of all ages pursuing sustained programs of learning independent of any educational provider.
5. Popular materials library: The library features current, high-demand, high-interest materials in a variety of formats for persons of all ages.
6. Preschoolers' door to learning: The library encourages young children to develop an interest in reading and learning through services for children, and for parents and children together.
7. Reference library: The library actively provides timely, accurate, and useful information for community residents.
8. Research center: The library assists scholars and researchers to conduct in-depth studies, investigate specific areas of knowledge, and create new knowledge.

Three more publications need to be mentioned to complete this historical survey of public library planning: *Output Measures for Public Library Services to Children: A Manual of Standardized Procedures* (1992), *Planning for Results: A Public Library Transformation Process* (1998), and *New Planning for Results* (2001). All were published by ALA.

Collection Development

Some mention needs to be made of collection development in public libraries during this period. The Public Library Inquiry at mid-twentieth century found that 10% of collections accounted for 90% of all use. The inquiry also found that 60% of public library users came in for leisure reading—primarily fiction. The same holds true 50 years later.

During the 1980s, there was a debate in the literature and at conferences over the question of demand versus quality. On one side were the proponents of supplying large quantities of copies of books in demand at the expense of purchasing fewer of the little-used books. Others felt that the emphasis should be on quality and that the public library should cultivate a more serious reading level. The majority of librarians were somewhere in the middle.

Public library collection development became a specialized area beginning with the mid-1970s and included selection, deselection, evaluation, arrangement, and marketing of the collections. In recent years, some public libraries have followed the model of the megabookstores with eye-catching displays and coffee—unheard of in the past.

During the 1960s and 1970s, public libraries adopted multimedia formats into their collections and, beginning in the 1990s, moved rapidly into providing music CDs, audiobooks, and films—first on video and later on DVD—as high-circulation items. As an example, the Iowa State Library reported that during 2005 26% of all circulation in Iowa public libraries was for video-audio titles.

But total public library collections were still weighted heavily toward books and serials as seen from this NCES data for 2002:

Books and Serial Volumes	785,075,000
Audio/Video and Film	64,466,000
Serial Subscriptions	1,946,000

Adult Services

During 1941–1956, the main force of public library adult services was strengthening democracy, promoting an enlightened citizenship, and assisting in the realization of democratic ideals. That was during the period of WWII and the Cold War that followed, along with the Korean War. This was also the period of book and audiovisual (AV) programs (primarily film) and discussion and forum programs such as the Great Issues program, the American Heritage Project, and the Great Books program. Helen Lyman's groundbreaking study of adult education activities at U.S. public libraries was published by ALA in 1954.

Lyman's *Adult Education Activities in Public Libraries* was the first survey of its kind about the types of group services offered by public libraries and state library extension agencies during 1952–1953. About 55% of libraries surveyed were actively engaged in providing such services, with the following activities being the most prominent: exhibits and displays inside and outside of the library, book talks, advice and participation in program planning, publicizing and informing about adult education activities, and providing physical space. The survey called for the need to formulate a philosophy of library adult education and for better training of adult service librarians.

By the beginning of the 1950s, the "Readers' Advisory" concept that had been so strong in the pre-WWII period began to wane. There was no time for individually prepared readers' lists—though standard lists of popular topics were still issued. The term "readers' guidance" replaced "readers' advisor," reflecting a shift in emphasis and a dispersal of the readers' advisory function. The adult services librarian and/or reference and information service librarian took over the role of the readers' advisor.

The ALA Library Community Project of 1955 emphasized adult service based on community needs and cooperation with other agencies, as well as services and programs for groups. From 1957–1991, the emphasis was on literacy and basic adult education. Federal funding in 1956, 1960, and 1964, President Johnson's War on Poverty, the Adult Education Act of 1966—all had an impact, particularly on public library assistance to the new urban residents, rural Appalachia and southern poor whites, rural African Americans, and migrant workers from Mexico and Central America.

The public library was promoted as a community information center in the 1970s and as an important source for literacy. With the help of federal funding, information and referral centers were established at libraries in Atlanta, Cleveland, Detroit, Houston, and Queens.

During the 1980s, the National Endowment for the Humanities began to provide funding to public librarians for projects and programs in conjunction with scholars and writers, and about books and poetry. NEH and ALA jointly sponsored many reading and discussion programs such as "Let's Talk about It" and "Voices and Visions."

Public libraries continued to expand services to special population groups—particularly from the 1960s onward. "Outreach programs" was a term that first appeared in 1970–1971 (in *Library Literature*). By the turn of the century, the following special population groups were listed in *Library Literature* index showing the extent of these outreach services:

Minorities	Immigrants	Homeless
Asian Americans	Handicapped	Poor
Black	Blind	Unemployed Job Seekers
Spanish-American	Institutionalized	Illiterate
Native American	Prison	Migrant Workers
Multicultural Groups	Shut-ins	Business Community
Ethnic Groups	Parents	Labor
Foreign-Born	Seniors	

The reference and adult services division had a project from 1983–1986 that provided libraries with planning and benchmarking information and resulted in a publication entitled *Adult Services in the Eighties*—an update of Lyman's 1954 survey—by Kathleen McCook.

The most frequent services provided were individual and group library instruction, displays and exhibits, interlibrary loan, maintenance of community activity information files, provisions of reading lists or bibliographies, referral to other agencies for literacy education, circulation of musical recordings, and library-sponsored programs.

Readers' advisory service experienced a renaissance in the 1990s. It had never completely gone away—during the 1970s, it had resurfaced as learner's advisory service—but now it was back. One cause may have been the ALA's planning and role-setting designation of public libraries as popular materials centers. Other causes were growing numbers of popular books being published, many new guides to fiction and genre, computerized guides to reading, and numerous websites sponsored by libraries that provided adult readers guidance, which were updated and interactive. Along with this came the popularity of adult reading clubs and Oprah's emphasis on reading on her television program.

Services to Children and Young Adults

By the mid-twentieth century, children's work in public libraries had already developed traditional services that continue to this day: a quality book collection (now including other media), a story hour, a pre-school story hour, reference and reader's advisory services for children and parents, a summer reading club, and close contacts with area schools and community organizations.

As school libraries began to grow and develop in the 1960s and 1970s on the elementary level, they took over some of the tasks of stimulating and guiding young readers as well as providing curriculum support. Children's service in public libraries shifted more support to pre-school and summer activities.

During the 1980s and 1990s, new challenges occurred with the increasing numbers of single parents and with both parents working. There was the problem of "latchkey" children left in public libraries. There were also parents who were homeschooling their children and depending on public library support. Some public libraries began providing homework support for children and young adults in regular school. Finally, there was the growing diversity of young library users—including children of newly arrived immigrants.

Young adult services in the post–World War II period began with *Public Library Plans for the Teen Age* (1948), which outlined typical services for youth such as reading guidance, group activities, reference service, educational and vocational guidance, cooperation with all adults working with or interested in young people, and cooperation with schools. The report also discussed book collections and set some standards for service to young adults.

ALA's *Young Adult Services in the Public Library* (1960) stressed organization and administration, selection of materials, and reading guidance. The social changes in the mid and late 1960s shifted the focus from book-centered to program-centered service, with outreach attempts to bring in more young people who ordinarily did not use libraries. Film programs became popular in the 1970s.

In 1977, *Directions for Library Service to Young Adults* was a conservative document stressing fairly traditional services such as referral, readers' advisory programs, outreach and publicity, selection of materials in different formats, and administrative matters.

Beginning in the 1980s, specialized library service to adolescents seemed to be in a decline. Many of the special rooms and alcoves set up in the 1930s and the 1940s to serve young adults specifically and separately had been removed or closed. Students continued to use public libraries in great numbers but were more often served by generalist librarians.

The most recent National Center for Educational Statistics (1995) provides key data on *Services and Resources for Children and Young Adults in Public Libraries* as of fall 1993. Of the 18 million people entering public libraries during a typical week in the fall of 1993, 60% were children and young adults. Thirty percent of all public librarians who provide service directly to the public specialized in services to children, young adults, or both. Thirty-nine percent of libraries employed a children's librarian, 11% employed a young adult librarian, and 24% had a youth services specialist on the staff. Eleven percent had neither a young adult collection nor a young adult section, but 58% had a young adult room or area housing the young adult collection. The remaining libraries shelved young adult materials with the adult collection (15%) or in the children's area (11%). Librarians reported that insufficient librarian staff was the leading barrier to increasing services and resources for both children and young adults.

Children's service in public libraries remains vital and continues to grow, as seen by the NCES data, as shown in table 2.1.

Table 2.1.   Children's Circulation and Program Attendance at Public Libraries

Circulation

1993	462.9 million (29% of total circulation)
2002	682.9 million (36% of total circulation)

Program Attendance

1993	35.6 million
2002	52.1 million

Public Libraries Today

Let us see how far public libraries have come since World War II. The latest data from the National Center for Educational Statistics is shown in table 2.2.

The latest data from the Library Research Center at the University of Illinois shows that the Index of American Public Library Circulation rose from 100 in 2000 to 112 for 2004.

Table 2.2.   9,137 Public Libraries Surveyed, 2002

Holdings

2002	785.1 million books and serial volumes (2.8 vols. per capita)
	35.7 million audio
	28.7 million video
	1.96 million serial subscriptions
2001	2,324,000 electronic format (CD-ROM, magnetic tapes, disks)

Circulation

1990	1,400,000	5.75 per capita
2002	1,900,000	6.8 per capita

Visits

1990	507,000	3.13 per capita
2002	1,200,000	4.5 per capita

Reference Transactions

1990	201,414,485	0.9 per capita
2002	301,800,000	1.1 per capita

Bookmobiles

2002	873
1991	1,125 (highest)
1950	603

Other 2002 Data

98% of the U.S population had access to public library services
81% of public libraries had one single direct service outlet
19% had more than one—e.g., branch or bookmobile
76% were members of a system, federation, or cooperative service

Income	$8.6 billion, $30.97 per capita
	78% from local sources
	12% from state
	1% from federal
	9% other—gifts, interest, fines, fees
Expenditures	65% staff, 136,890 FTE staff (22% were MLS librarians)
	14% collections

In 2005, ALA commissioned a study by KRC Research and Consulting to measure usage of public libraries. Here are the results:

- Two-thirds of adults (about 135,000,000) visited their public libraries and have library cards.

- Seven out of ten were extremely or very satisfied with their public library—up 10% from a 2002 survey.
- Eighty-five percent agreed that their public library needed more funding.
- About 92% of respondents believed libraries will be needed in the future.

Since the 2002 survey, the use of services has grown in almost every category:

- Borrowing books—up 14%
- Consulting with librarians—up 7%
- Taking out CDs, videos, and computer software—up 13%
- Attending library programs—up 8%

Some 96% agreed that because public libraries provide free access they play an important role in giving everyone a chance to succeed.

In 1996, the W. K. Kellogg Foundation funded a report by the Benton Foundation on public libraries and the challenge they face in the digital world. The study found that Americans continue to "have a love affair" with their libraries but they were having difficulty deciding where libraries fit in the new digital world. The report said there was good reason for optimism, since strong public sentiment already favored key visions for the future of libraries. Libraries and their leaders were challenged to chart a role for themselves, giving meaning and message to their future institutions and central role in community life. Now almost 10 years later, it seems that they have met the challenge. Public libraries are being used more than ever both in and from outside of their buildings. Public library websites provide widespread service. The innovative Internet Public Library, developed in 1995 at the School of Information of the University of Michigan, was a forerunner on the Internet. But people of all ages are still coming in to use the library even though they have computer access in their homes and at work. The future of the public library seems secure.

THE RISE OF THE SCHOOL LIBRARY MEDIA CENTER

School libraries changed dramatically during this period. They grew in numbers from about 14,000 in 1948 to over 98,000 in 2004. Their collections changed from being book centered to multimedia, justifying a new name, *school library media center*. The role of the school librarian also changed to a more dynamic library media specialist, much more involved as a partner in the teaching process.

It all began with the 1945 publication by ALA of *School Libraries for Today and Tomorrow: Functions and Standards*. But the real change occurred after the Soviet Union launched the first satellite, Sputnik, into orbit. Americans feared that the Soviets had passed the United States in the space race. In 1958, Congress approved the National Defense Education Act (NDEA), which provided funds for training and retraining teachers and strengthening science, foreign language, and mathematics instruction in the public schools. School libraries benefited by receiving funds to strengthen their collections in these areas.

A U.S. Office of Education report published in 1960 and entitled *Public School Library Statistics, 1958–59* noted that about one half of the nation's schools had no library and that well over one half did not have the services of a qualified librarian. Even in schools with libraries, collections averaged fewer than five books per student. Two thirds of elementary schools were without school libraries.

The 1960s began a period of tremendous growth in school library programs throughout the nation. New standards, federal funding, and foundation support were very influential in promoting and strengthening school libraries.

The year 1960 saw the ALA publication of *Standards for School Library Programs* by the American Association of School Librarians, in cooperation with 19 other professional associations. These standards stressed the responsibility of school boards, administrators, and supervisory personnel in developing successful school library programs. In addition to their national impact, these standards influenced the development and expansion of state and local standards by providing quantitative recommendations on the wide variety of services that a school library should perform.

Just a year later, the Council on Library Resources funded an eighteen-month school library development project aimed at developing school library leadership to implement national standards.

In 1963, school library growth was accelerated though the Knapp School Libraries Project (1963–1974). ALA used funds provided by the Knapp Foundation to set up a three-pronged program that had a tremendous national impact on selling the need for quality school library programs to the public. The Knapp project set up model school library media centers throughout the country. It funded the School Library Manpower Project (1968–1974), which developed school library job descriptions and manpower needs. And it set up six model library education programs for school library media specialists at Arizona State, Auburn, Mankato State, Millersville State, the University of Denver, and the University of Michigan. Thousands of educators visited the model demonstration centers and thousands of others learned of them through written reports and through viewing a specially produced film called *And Something More.*

The lobbying efforts of ALA and the efforts of key school librarians across the country resulted in the passage of the Elementary and Secondary Education Act (ESEA) in 1965. Funds were placed in Title II specifically to purchase library materials. These funds were then combined with local initiatives and volunteer efforts to build school libraries in elementary buildings and to expand libraries in secondary schools.

The effect of Knapp Foundation and federal funding was phenomenal—thousands of new libraries were either founded or greatly expanded. The demand for librarians exceeded the supply. Although federal support has waned with the times, some level of support continues to this date.

In 1969, the first joint standards cooperatively produced by AASL and DAVI (Department of Audio Visual Instruction of the National Education Association) were issued as *Standards for School Media Programs.* In addition to emphasizing the advantages that unified media programs could bring and providing quantitative guidelines, the standards stressed the necessity of fusing facilities and services.

Another set of standards issued in 1975 was *Media Programs: District and School.* After reaffirming the unified approaches to centralizing all forms of media and media services in schools, the 1975 standards also stressed the media center's role in planning and executing the school's instructional program rather than being simply a passive support service.

In 1978, a "Report of the Task Force on the Role of the School Library Media Programs in Networking" made a key recommendation that school library programs participate in library networks in every region, state, and area in the nation.

In 1981, the American Association of School Librarians began the publication of *School Media Quarterly* (later changed to *School Library Media Quarterly*). Back in 1974, R. R. Bowker had already begun to publish *School Library Journal* as a separate publication from *Library Journal*.

In 1988, new guidelines, as opposed to the previous standards, for school library media programs were published by ALA but jointly prepared by AALS and AECT. *Information Power: Guidelines for School Library Media Programs* described the school media specialist serving as a proactive initiator and participative partner with other educators as a member of an instructional team. The school media specialists had three roles: teacher, information specialist, and instructional consultant.

In the mid-1990s, the DeWitt-Wallace/Reader's Digest Foundation funded a $40 million initiative to create model elementary and middle school libraries. This Library Power Project, which was administered by the American Association of School Librarians, included nineteen sites that were provided funding over a three-year period to increase their collections, train staff, and improve facilities. Schools were required to commit to full-time library media specialists, maintain a flexible library schedule, and encourage collaboration between teachers and library media specialists.

The 1998 *Information Power: Building Partnerships for Learning* indicated that the mission of the library media programs was to ensure that students and staff are effective users of ideas and information. This was to be accomplished as follows:

- by providing intellectual and physical access to materials in all formats
- by providing instruction to foster competence and stimulate interest in reading, viewing, and using information and ideas.
- by working with other educators to design learning strategies to meet the needs of individual students.

In 2001, the Bush administration's No Child Left Behind program was approved by Congress and began providing seventy to ninety grants per year ($12.5 million) for school library media centers in its Literacy through School Libraries provision.

In July 2002, Laura Bush hosted a White House Conference on School Libraries to discuss the latest research on libraries, student achievement, and successful programs. The conference called attention to the critical role that school libraries played in children's academic success. In 2003, 132 school libraries shared $640,000 in grants from the Laura Bush Foundation to purchase books for their collections. In 2004, there was $660,000 in grants to 136 school libraries.

School libraries have come a long way since the late 1940s and particularly since the 1960s. As a category, they were far ahead of other academic, public, and special libraries in embracing all forms of information media. They have also been quick to adopt the advances in computer and communication technology. With over 98,000 school library media centers and 62,000 librarians and 93,000 other staff, they far surpass the other types of libraries in numbers. Most importantly, the school library media centers of today play a far more important education role than the school library of the 1940s.

But there is still room for progress. The latest data provided for 1999–2000 showed that 91.6% of public schools had a school library media center. Only 62.6% of private schools had such a center. The percentage of schools with a paid, state-certified library media specialist was 75.2% in public schools (57,781) and only 20.2% in private schools (3,441).

ACADEMIC LIBRARIES

This overview of academic and research libraries is presented in a number of sections. First is a chronological review in two parts: one from 1945 to the mid-1970s, and a second from the mid-1970s to the present. There will also be separate sections on collection development and bibliographic instruction in academic libraries, and finally a statistical look at academic libraries at the turn of the century.

World War II to the Mid-1970s

The progress and growth of academic libraries from 1945 to the early 1970s was truly amazing, as was the growth of their host institutions of higher education. Higher education enrollment went from 2,300,000 in 1950, to 3,600,000 in 1960, to 8,650,000 in 1970. Universities added new professional schools and colleges and new and expanded doctoral programs. Four-year colleges also grew rapidly. Former teacher's colleges became colleges of arts and sciences and, at times, full-fledged universities. All added new majors and programs of study. Community college growth was astonishing, from 460 in 1946, to 521 in 1960, to 892 by 1970.

Libraries grew with their parent institutions, responding to more faculty and students, to new areas of study, and to the information explosion.

In 1952, the average total expenditure of each Association of Research Libraries (ARL) member was $478,980. In 1968, it was $2,866,922. The collections of these libraries averaged 928,052 printed books in 1952. By 1969, the average had almost doubled to 1,843,511.

In 1952, only fifteen university libraries in the United States had collections of more than one million volumes. By 1970, 58 libraries had reached this size.

The total number of volumes in all academic libraries went up from 215,000,000 in 1962–1963 to 315,000,000 in 1970–1971. Professional library staff for the same years went from 11,200 to 18,700.

Harvard University opened the first undergraduate library in 1949. The number of undergraduate libraries then increased to 10 by 1960, to 20 by 1965, and to 46 by 1970 (but decreased to 23 by 2004).

University libraries developed in other ways also. In 1948, over 50 research libraries joined together in the Farmington Plan in a major cooperative effort of coordinated foreign acquisitions through ARL. The goals was to bring to this country at least one copy of every monograph of research interest published anywhere in the world through a system of assigning to individual libraries responsibility for specific subjects and specific geographical areas.

In 1949, the Midwest Interlibrary Center was established and in 1965 became the Center for Research Libraries. It had been originally formed by 10 midwestern university libraries with a program for joint buying and centralized storage of less-used materials.

Standards for academic libraries began to be developed at this time. First there was *Standards for College Libraries* in 1959. In 1975, these standards were broadened to include staff and space as well as collections. *Standards for Junior College Libraries* was published in 1960 and then in 1972 superseded by *Guidelines for Two-year College and Learning Resources Program.* There was a strong movement toward the community or junior college library becoming a learning resource center, embracing all formats of media as well as media-viewing and production facilities. This was easier to accomplish since many of these libraries were newly established.

The 1960s also saw great progress in the attainment of faculty rank, or at least faculty status, by academic librarians. In 1956, the American Association of University Professors (AAUP) gave such recognition to academic librarians. By 1966, over 51% of academic librarians were said to have faculty status. The percentage continued to climb into the 1970s (75% by 1976). In 1975, ACRL published *Faculty Status for Academic Libraries*, a collection of policy statements in support of faculty status.

Faculty status was to have advantages and disadvantages and was not necessarily accepted with enthusiasm by all academic librarians. In most instances, it did not mean ten-month appointments with traditional faculty ranks and pay, but it often meant an expectation of research and scholarly publications when it was time for review for promotion and/or tenure by library faculty who did not have the flexible time to support such activity. At the same time, however, it was a recognition of the important role that librarians were playing in the academic environment.

Federal funding had a positive impact on academic libraries beginning in the 1960s. First there was the Academic Facilities Act of 1963, which funded construction of academic library buildings, including libraries at both public and private institutions. In 1964, Title III of the Library Services and Construction Act provided local, regional, state, or interstate cooperation networks for information service among all types of libraries including academic, public, school, and special libraries and information centers. But the greatest impact came from the Higher Education Act of 1965. Title II-A granted funds for acquisitions and networking to college libraries. Title II-C was targeted at research libraries by granting funds for collection development in subject areas of national importance.

From the late 1960s and into the 1970s, a number of key developments occurred that set the stage for the 1975-to-date section of our coverage. In 1967, OCLC was founded by Frederick Kilgour as a consortium of 49 academic libraries in the state of Ohio. Its primary purpose was resource sharing and a reduction in the per-unit cost of cataloging. We have already seen that MARC was also developed at this time. And in the same year, Stanford University began "Bibliographic Automation of Large Library Operations Using a Time-Sharing Unit System" (BALLOTS).

In 1974, the Research Libraries Group (RLG) was founded as an alternative to institutional self-sufficiency during a time of tremendous publishing output and rising costs. This consortium originally consisted of Columbia, Harvard, Yale, and the New York Public Library. A few years later, Stanford joined the Research Libraries Group and its BALLOTS network was renamed the Research Library Information Network RLIN.

The Mid-1970s to Date

By the mid-1970s, higher education was in trouble. The Vietnam War, an energy crisis, a downturn in the economy that included both inflation and a recession, plus a slowdown in enrollments brought about budget reductions and cutbacks. Academic libraries were also affected by financial stringency.

But the academic libraries also began to have dramatic changes in their structure, services, and collection policies. First it should be noted that *Standards for University Libraries* was published in 1979. Then there was the impact of technology and library automation. The introduction of online processing system, the appearance of OPACs, and the availability of integrated systems supporting an array of library processes were revolutionary.

Bibliographic utilities such as RLG and WLN and especially OCLC had a great impact on academic libraries. OCLC systems transformed the cataloging of collections, access to bibliographic data, and interlibrary loan. OCLC also played a key role in the development of seventeen regional consortia such as NELINET and SOLINET. (There is more on this in the next chapter.)

From the 1970s to the present, academic library management was transformed from a hierarchical and autocratic model to one that was more participative and democratic. More women began serving as directors of academic libraries. The Association of Research Libraries sponsored, designed, and administered a variety of programs to improve the management of large academic libraries through MRAP, Management Review and Analysis Program. The Council of Library Resources provided excellent opportunities for leadership roles through the CLR Management Intern Program and the Senior Fellowship Program.

The 1990s brought the Internet and the Web to academic libraries and the migration of students to the Web. Library websites became very important, and along with them, new positions such as Webmaster. Bibliographic instructions became increasingly Web-based. Electronic (e-mail or Web-based) reference service was made available. More and more space was allocated within libraries for computer labs.

Acquisitions and subscriptions to full-text electronic documents began to grow rapidly, as did expenditures for electronic resources. Reference tools and especially indexes were being replaced by electronic versions. Librarians were also working with faculty to help them incorporate electronic resources into their courses. There was also a shift from microfilm to digital records for preservation. Indeed, this concept of remote access to information from the Web by way of networks was revolutionizing library service.

The spread of distance learning by many academic institutions brought a reaction from academic libraries as they attempted to provide off-campus students with free interlibrary loan and/or document delivery service.

In summary, a shift from an emphasis on ownership to access became the main driving force by the end of the 1990s.

In 2000, new *Standards for College Libraries* were approved. Their emphasis was on outcomes assessments as a basis for measuring library effectiveness. In 2004, the Association of College and Research Libraries approved new standards for all types of libraries in higher education. Libraries were to establish individual goals, focus on the library's contribution to the institution's effectiveness and student learning outcomes, and then to make comparisons with peer groups.

Collection Development

Up until the early 1950s, book selection in academic libraries was primarily the responsibility of faculty members. There was a shift as faculty members got too busy with research and increasing numbers of students and as academic librarians became more professional and received faculty status. Subject bibliographers were also being appointed on library staffs.

Responding to the increasing role of academic librarians in selection, *Choice* began publication in 1964, reviewing in each issue several hundred new books of a scholarly or academic nature of greatest interest to college libraries, faculty, and students. *Choice* magazine was launched by ALA's Association of College and Research Libraries (ACRL) with the assistance of a major grant from the Council of Library Resources (CLR).

Until the 1970s, collection development was marked by an explosive growth in academic and research library collections, by a growing variety of information formats, and by an increasing awareness of the need for interlibrary cooperation.

From the 1970s to the present was a period of economic constraints, of a rapidly growing digital environment, of increasing cooperation, and of the serials crisis. The serials crisis hit academic libraries in the mid-1980s as subscription costs of certain scholarly journals began rising at unprecedented rates. The prices of many scientific, medical, and technical journals were increasing by 50% or more per year. Publishers of these journals decided to view scholarly information as an economic commodity rather than the result of researchers' work. There were a number of results. More was being spent by libraries for serials and less was spent for monographs. NCES data from 2002–2003 shows that all academic libraries spent $512,076,817 for print and electronic serials that year, while the amount for books was $267,260,940. There were periodic waves of journal cancellations by research libraries. At the same time, budgets for acquisitions were not rising and in some cases shrinking. The crisis continues for both print and online journals.

Many research libraries realized that no one library can provide all of the material needed by its patrons and that cooperative action was needed to address collection development practices.

Beginning in the late 1970s and through the 1980s, RLG collection development librarians created a mechanism for coordinating collection development in research libraries so that unnecessary and wasteful duplications could be avoided. The result of these efforts was the RLG Conspectus, which was then adopted by libraries beyond RLG in this country and abroad. But there was a shift in focus in the late 1990s from coordinated collections assessments to projects aimed at achieving greater collections access.

Another example of cooperation was the development of consortial buying groups, particularly for digital materials. OHIOLINK, a group of Ohio-based academic libraries, was an example of this. In 1997, OHIOLINK signed its first statewide agreement with Academic Press to provide all of their titles to all members of the consortium in full-text digital format.

New buying models were also developed. One was to obtain new books on approval plans under which the vendor would ship to the library on a regular basis all the books that matched the library's profile in each subject area. Still another procedure was to use commercial document delivery for low-used journals instead of subscribing to them.

Very significant was JSTOR, established as an independent not-for-profit organization in 1995 with support from the Mellon Foundation. Growing back files of print journal runs were creating space problems in research libraries. There was also the problem of degenerating paper. JSTOR provided digital backup files of such journals. As of January 9, 2006, there were 2,650 participating libraries from 98 countries with access to almost 20 million pages. During 2005, there were 241,210,494 journal issues accessed.

Finally we have the establishment of the Scholarly Publishing and Academic Resources Coalition (SPARC) in 1997, a self-supporting voluntary ARL initiative. Its purpose was to encourage competition in the scholarly communications market. SPARC has introduced new solutions to scientific journal publishing, facilitated the use of technology to expand access to scholarly information, and partnered with publishers to bring top-quality and low-cost research to a larger audience.

Bibliographic Instruction

This term *bibliographic instruction* is now being replaced by names like *user education* or *information literacy*. Bibliographic instruction grew rapidly during the 1960s and 1970s. The great influx of students, the publishing explosion, and the rapid growth of libraries were of concern to librarians who wanted to provide this special assistance to students. Another motivation may have been as a justification to attain faculty rank or status. Bibliographic instruction was, in essence, teaching.

During the mid-1960s, Patricia Knapp led the Monteith Library Project at Wayne State University. The main finding was that library competence was a liberal art that was ignored by a faculty intent on imparting content rather than competence in learning. Since faculty were subject specialists ignoring the library, it was important for the librarian to intervene and teach library competence. Knapp, along with Evan Farber at Earlham College Library, promoted course-integrated library and information resource instructions in partnership with faculty.

The Library College idea was first developed by Louis Shores in the 1930s and was reconsidered from the mid-1960s to the mid-1970s. Proponents felt that books and reading were the core of learning and that the best approach to independent study pursued in the library would be under the guidance of teacher/librarians who were both a subject master and bibliographic expert in all media formats. Convocations to discuss theory and implementation were held in 1965 and 1966. Although no true library college was ever begun, aspects were tried as experiments at Monteith, Stephens, and Earlham Colleges. *Library-College Journal* (later *Learning Today*) began in 1968 but ended in 1984.

In 1972, the Library Orientation Exchange (LOEX) was founded as a nonprofit, self-supporting educational clearinghouse. The first conference was held in 1973 and continues annually to this day. The LOEX borrowing collection consisted of print materials such as one-page handouts, bibliographies, and subject guides; instructional videos and audio tapes; and CD-ROMS.

Bibliographic instruction (BI) librarians were very enthusiastic and committed to their cause. By 1973, they formed an ALA Round Table (now the Library Instruction Round Table). By 1977, a Bibliographic Instruction Section was created within the ACRL. BI librarians were flooding the library press with articles and by 1983 created their own journal—*Research Strategies: A Journal of Library Concepts and Instruction.*

The development of academic library instruction has been dramatically affected by the emergence of new information technologies during the past twenty-five years. The replacement of card catalogs by online catalogs, the introduction of electronic versions of reference sources, and the advent of the Internet and the World Wide Web changed the way of library instruction and made it more important than ever.

The entire concept of academic librarians as teachers has been criticized by some from early in the twentieth century to the present. Most criticisms seemed to focus on three concerns: that library instruction is not a valid function of reference service and does not fit the library mission of providing information to patrons; that library instruction does not succeed in educating patrons; and that librarians do not fit well in the academic model of classroom teacher. But the great majority academic librarians think otherwise, and the instructional librarians are fervent and missionary-like in their beliefs and actions.

It should be noted that in the late 1980s and early 1990s, accreditation agencies began to include bibliographic instruction in their standards for academic libraries. The Middle States Commission on Higher Education in 1989 and the Southern Association of Colleges and Schools in 1992 strongly supported the need for a continuous program of bibliographic instruction.

In recent years, a new approach was proposed, called information literacy (IL), which is different from bibliographic instruction. While BI is based in the physical library, IL has no physical restraints. While BI has been tool based, IL is concept based. BI is focused on the mechanics of use, while IL helps people learn how to learn. BI has usually been connected with course requirements, while IL supports learning outcomes of academic programs.

Recent Data on Academic Libraries

And so for the year 2000 (the latest data available), the National Center for Educational Statistics reported that we had 3,923 institutions of higher education with 15,313,000 students, which is up from 2,300,000 in 1950 and 8,650,000 in 1970. Their libraries held 913,546,999 books and bound serials and government documents, 1,111,496,736 microform units, and 87,558,471 audiovisual material units, including video, film, and audio.

Other impressive statistics are:

- 194 million circulation transactions
- 9.5 million interlibrary loan transactions
- 16.5 million visitors per week
- 1.6 million reference transactions in a typical week
- 432,000 presentations to 7.5 million persons
- 96,555 FTE staff (31,036 professional FTE)
- $5 billion in expenditures
- $2.5 billion on staff (50% of expenditures)
- $1.1 billion on paper and electronic serial subscriptions (23% of expenditures)
- $552,000,000 on books and serial volumes (11% of expenditures)

It should be noted that the 568 doctoral-granting institution libraries (16% of total) spent 65% of all expenditures.

Finally, 94% of libraries provided access from within the library to an electronic catalog of library holdings, 99% provided Internet access within the library, and 73% provided library reference service by e-mail.

LIBRARY OF CONGRESS

Special attention must be paid to a review of the Library of Congress (LC) in the postwar period since it played a key role in library development as our de facto national library. LC celebrated its centennial in the year 2000. It is the largest library in the world, with 29 million books, 2.7 million recordings, 12 million photographs, 4.8 million maps, and 58 million manuscripts.

Archibald MacLeish resigned as Librarian of Congress in 1944. President Harry Truman named Assistant Librarian Luther H. Evans in his place, who served until 1953. In 1954, President Dwight D. Eisenhower named L. Quincy Mumford, who was director of the Cleveland Public Library, as Librarian of Congress and the only professionally trained librarian who has served in this post since 1945.

In 1957, Mumford began planning for a third major building. In his 20 years in office, he guided the library through an intensive period of national and international expansion through increased federal funding.

Most dramatic was the growth of the foreign acquisitions program bought with the U.S.-owned foreign currency under the terms of the Agricultural Trade Development and Assistance Act of 1954. In 1965, Title II-C of the Higher Education Act directed the Library of Congress to acquire all current library materials of value to scholarship published throughout the world and to provide cataloging information for their materials promptly after they have been acquired. This was called the National Program for Acquisitions and Cataloging (NPAC), and its first office was opened in London in 1966.

We have already mentioned the contribution of the LC in the creation of the MARC format for communicating bibliographic data in machine-readable form. The MARC format structure became the official national standard in 1971 and an international standard by 1973. Mention will be made elsewhere of the important work of the LC in the preservation and conservation of library collections.

In 1975, President Gerald R. Ford appointed Daniel J. Boorstin as Librarian of Congress. He was a former director of what is now the Museum of American History. Both funding and visibility of the Library of Congress increased under his administration. The move into the Madison Building provided much-needed space relief. The Center for the Book (a part of the LC designed to promote books, reading, libraries, and literacy) was established in 1977.

Historian James H. Billington was appointed Librarian of Congress by President Ronald Reagan in 1987. In 1994, the library made its bibliographic records and selected works from its American collections available electronically and began establishing what is now a multi-tiered presence on the World Wide Web. In the same year, Congress approved the library's National Digital Library Program, which began collecting digital versions of historical materials from more than 70 collections in the library and in 33 other research institutions. Today, the LC is a leader in making its collections and information available on the Web—one of the most frequently used sites in the world, with 218 million hits in 2004.

SPECIAL LIBRARIES

Special libraries grew from 2,489 (including those in Canada) in 1953 to almost 10,000 in 2004, according to the *American Library Directory.*

The *Directory of Special Libraries and Information Centers* for 2004 has a listing of 16,496 in the United States and 2,723 in Canada. Membership in the Special Libraries Association went from 3,491 in 1944 to over 12,000 in 2004.

Beginning with the late 1940s, there was an explosion of scientific information that increased the number of scientific and technical libraries and placed a greater emphasis on the acquisition of journals and technical reports for their currency.

There was also a growing awareness of the global environment and of information as a commodity. The expenses associated with information acquisition and delivery were being examined, as was the value of information provided.

By the 1950s, a new breed of information specialists was in evidence — the documentalists, who already had formed the American Documentation Institute (ADI) in 1937. They felt that they were different from special librarians and insisted that a new profession was needed to cope with the proliferation of scientific information sources and the information storage and retrieval systems needed to provide access to them. Their emphasis was on subject knowledge and technological expertise in information systems. This was not what the schools of library science that were training special librarians were teaching at that time. Although many special librarians worked with scientific and technical information, the Special Libraries Association (SLA) also represented librarians in business and in many nonscience libraries. There was talk of the merger of ADI and SLA and there were members who belonged to both, but the differences were too great. The ADI became the American Society for Information Science in 1968 and now has 4,000 members.

In 1964, *Objectives and Standards for Special Libraries* was published by SLA. The 1960s and 1970s also brought the appearance of independent information providers, popularly called *information brokers*. They were often used by organizations and companies that could not or did not want to establish their own special library.

During the 1980s, electronic and telecommunications technology made it possible for special librarians to share information resources with off-site clients, with other libraries, and with the world at large.

The 1990s brought the Internet and the World Wide Web and concepts such as managing knowledge, collecting information to help successful competition, and providing networks of databases. Global competition made it necessary to acquire information on competitors, on regulations, and on the industry at large. The special library became thought of less as a place and more as an information service. There is some reflection of this in the journal articles of that period.

At the same time, there has been a drop in the membership of special libraries in the United States as reported by *The American Library Directory*, and shown in table 2.3.

Table 2.3.   Number of Special Libraries

	1993/1994	2005/2006
Special Libraries	10,149	8,208
Special Libraries*	11,257	9,526

*including those in public and academic libraries and in government and the armed forces

One cause for the above decline may be the downsizing and outsourcing that began in the mid-1990s among companies and corporations. There is some reflection of this on special libraries in the journal articles of that period. Special libraries in the nonprofit agencies also often faced cutbacks as their parent institutions received less support.

Today's special librarians are very different from those in the 1940s. They may not even be called librarians. They are often involved in the vision, goals, and values of their patron and/or organization. They try to anticipate information needs. There is usually a collaborative relationship between the librarian and the information customer. Today's special librarians do more than just locate and collect data and information. They add value to the information by evaluating and analyzing it, by packaging it, and by presenting it in a way to maximize its usefulness.

The Special Libraries Association has continued to evolve with the times. In 1985, its headquarters moved from New York City to Washington, D.C. In 1996, "Competencies for Special Librarians of the 21st Century" was published. In 1997, its longtime official journal *Special Libraries* was discontinued but replaced in 1998 by *Information Outlook*. SLA has also become much more an international organization with members in 83 countries. The association has grown to 58 regional chapters, 23 divisions, and 11 caucuses. The divisions range from engineering and advertising/marketing, to military librarians, to solo librarians and museum libraries—art and humanities.

Along with the drop in special libraries, there has also been a drop in membership, as shown in the *Bowker Annual of Library and Book Trade.* Membership seemed to have peaked at 14,500 in 1997 and remained at that level until the 2001 annual. The 2002 and 2003 annuals (with data for previous years) show membership down to 13,500. The current SLA website states that there are over 12,000 members—all of this as membership has expanded worldwide.

During the 2003 SLA conference, membership voted against a measure that would have changed the organization name to Information Professional International—but the voting was only 71 votes short of the needed two-thirds majority.

In 2003, the 1996 "Competencies for Special Librarians of the 21st Century" were reissued as "Competencies for Information Professionals of the 21st Century." The following statements are taken directly from the 2003 revision:

An information professional (IP) strategically uses information in his/her job to advance the mission of the organization. IP's include, but are not limited to librarians, knowledge managers, chief information officers, web developers, information brokers and consultants. . . .

Information organizations are defined as those entities that deliver information-based solutions to a given market. . . .

The four professional competencies are: managing information organization, managing information resources, managing information services, and applying information tools and technologies. . . .

Personal competencies represent a set of attitudes, skills and values that enable practitioners to work effectively and contribute positively to their organizations, clients and profession. These competencies range from being strong communicators, to demonstrating the value-add of their contributions, to remaining flexible and positive in an ever-changing environment.

Finally, core competencies are described as "information professionals [who] contribute to the knowledge base of the profession by sharing best practices and experiences, and continue to learn about information products, services, and management practices throughout the life of his/her career; and information professionals commit to professional excellence and ethics, and to the values and principles of the profession."

In 2004, the SLA board of directors voted to "Do Business as SLA," meaning that as an organizations "SLA" will be used instead of the Special Libraries Association. This was not a legal name change. One major justification was that many information professionals outside of North America were unfamiliar with the term "special libraries" and hesitated to join the organization. With this model, new market segments throughout the world will be attracted to the organization.

Indeed, there are many other types of "special libraries" that are not part of SLA and for which little coverage is provided in this study. Most have their own professional associations. Among these are medical libraries, which by 2004 totaled 2,135; law libraries (968); government libraries (1,225); and military libraries (314). As an example of growth, there were 351 government libraries in 1954.

THE ESTABLISHMENT AND GROWTH OF PRESIDENTIAL LIBRARIES

Presidential libraries are an example of the many special types of libraries that were established after World War II.

It was President Franklin D. Roosevelt who started it all. He donated the land, built the library building with private funding, and then gave the library and his papers to the National Archives. The library was dedicated on June 30, 1941, at Hyde Park, New York. It became the model for the Presidential Library System. Privately constructed and donated to the government, presidential libraries provide assistance to researchers, expansive collections of presidential materials, and a museum experience for hundreds of thousands of visitors each year.

President Harry S. Truman followed the same pattern when he decided in 1950 on a presidential library in his hometown of Independence, Missouri.

Dwight D. Eisenhower's support of the development of a library at the site of the already established Eisenhower Museum in Abilene, Kansas, prompted Congress to pass the Presidential Libraries Act of 1955. This act provided continuing legal authority for the government to accept the gift of a presidential library without seeking legislative authority for each new library.

President Herbert Hoover had originally given his papers to Stanford University, but responded favorably to a request of a citizens' committee from his hometown for the development of a library in West Branch, Iowa. His library became the third added to the system in 1962. The Eisenhower Library was also opened in 1962.

Over time, the location for presidential libraries shifted from the president's hometown to a larger metropolitan area or a university campus. The Lyndon B. Johnson Presidential Library and Museum became the first presidential library located on a university campus, at the University of Texas in Austin. The John F. Kennedy Library is adjacent to the University of Massachusetts in Boston. The Gerald Ford Library was established at the University of Michigan. The Jimmy Carter Library is near the campus of Emory University. The George Bush Library is part of Texas A&M University. The William Clinton Library is affiliated with the University of Arkansas at Little Rock.

With President Nixon's resignation in 1974, Congress enacted the Presidential Recordings and Materials Preservation Act to ensure that no evidence in his papers, tapes, and so forth relating to Watergate would be destroyed. The Nixon presidential materials were seized and given to the National Archives and Research Service. The Nixon Presidential Materials staff is located in College Park, Maryland. Not part of the presidential libraries was the Richard Nixon Library and Birthplace established privately in Yorba Linda, California. However, in January 2004, legislation was passed that made this a federally operated presidential library.

The presidential libraries do contain books and serials but also much more correspondence; photographs; motion picture film; disc, audiotape, and videotape recordings; museum objects; and e-mail messages. They also have exhibits; host conferences, lectures, and public forums; and sponsor educational programs.

STATE LIBRARY AGENCY GROWTH

By 1950, state library agencies were providing functions and services such as reference service to state legislative, executive, and judicial bodies; maintenance of archival and historical collections; special library service to the handicapped and institutionalized; extension library service to some unserved areas; and some form of guidance to library development in each state—particularly the encouragement of public library systems in the 1950s and 1960s.

The big change came with the passage of the 1956 Library Service Act, which channeled federal funding to state library agencies for distribution throughout each state. State library agencies began to have greater impact in library development and reached a constituency heretofore unserved.

After only three years of partial funding, 30,000,000 more rural people had access to library service and an additional 200 bookmobiles were on rural roads. State funding for rural library service increased by 54% while local funding went up by 45%. State libraries became stronger and more influential because of the success of these new programs, which had been proposed, implemented, and administered by them.

In 1963, the American Association of State Libraries passed a set of *Standards for Library Function at the State Level* that sought to identify common goals and functions and effective procedures to achieve them.

The 1964 Library Services and Construction Act extended federal aid beyond rural areas and made the state libraries even more important and powerful. They were able to obtain greater appropriations from their legislatures by an average of four dollars of state money to one dollar of federal money. A year later, Title III of the 1965 LSCA revision focused on interlibrary cooperation, which again was taken up by state library agencies as leaders in the promotion of sharing resources.

By the year 2003, state libraries had grown tremendously and were involved in a myriad of services. NCES data showed the following:

- Total books and serial volumes: 224 million
- Audio and video materials: 327,614
- Serial subscriptions: 65,464
- Uncataloged government documents: 26 million

Earlier 2000 NCES sources showed 4,053 FTE (full-time equivalent) positions with 1,262 of these held by librarians holding a master's of library science (MLS) degree. Total expenditures exceeded $1 billion, with about two thirds going to state aid for libraries. Almost all state library agencies planned or monitored the development of electronic networks and provided or facilitated library access to online databases through subscriptions, leases, licenses, consortial memberships, or agreements. Almost all facilitated or subsidized electronic access to the holdings of other libraries in their states though OCLC participation.

All state library agencies facilitated library access to the Internet in their states and had Internet workstations available for public use in their own facilities.

Finally, state library agencies provided a long list of library development services to public, academic, school, and special libraries in their states. Among these were administration of library services and technology grants, reference referral service, interlibrary loan referral service, administration of state aid and state certification, consulting services, continuing education, collection of library statistics, and statewide public relations, and library promotion programs. As can be seen, these recent services and activities have advanced considerably from those in the years immediately after World War II.

In this chapter, we have seen how the different types of libraries have evolved during the past sixty years—their differences and similarities and how they each made use of the core areas of the field covered in chapter 1. The next chapter shows how they began to cooperate and work together to form library systems, consortia, and networks for the common good.

CHAPTER 3

Library Cooperation:
Systems, Consortia, and Networks

This chapter traces the historic growth and impact of library cooperation since 1945 in general and then covers it in greater depth by examining three leading cooperative ventures: the Center for Research Libraries (CLR), the Online Computer Library Center (OCLC), and the Research Libraries Group (RLG). A comparative look at library cooperation in the Buffalo area in 1945 and in 2005 is also provided.

Library cooperation and networking were founded on the belief that the good of all transcends that of each individual entity, that librarianship could move ahead more effectively if all cooperate than if each goes alone. In the late 1940s, most libraries were stand-alone operations. Just forty years later, most libraries were members of one—and probably of more than one—system, consortia, or network.

In the postwar years, public libraries were the first to join together to form public library systems for more efficient use of resources and better service to users. The process began in New York State in the early 1950s and spread throughout the nation. By 1969, there were 491 such public library systems in the United States identified in a survey by Nelson Associates.

Regional union card catalogs had been started in the 1930s and 1940s to maintain bibliographic records in their respective regions to serve as interlibrary loan clearinghouses. After World War II, the practice of interlibrary borrowing moved from a privilege to a regularly expected part of the user's right to service.

The Midwest Interlibrary Loan Center (MILC) was an early example of library cooperation. It was founded in 1949 in Chicago by thirteen midwestern universities with four lofty goals: coordinated collection policies, centralized cataloguing, cooperatively stored little-used materials, and cooperative acquisitions. When the center opened for business in 1951, the cooperative acquisitions program began with subscriptions to forty newspapers on microfilm. The centralized cataloging and coordination of collection policies proved unworkable. We will see MILC's further growth later in this chapter as the Center for Research Libraries.

Beginning in the late 1960s, groups of libraries began banding together regionally to harness the power of the newly developed MARC records and communications protocol. Indeed, it was the availability of the machine-readable cataloging as a bibliographic record that made resource sharing possible not only in interlibrary loan but also in cataloging and even cooperative collection development.

Two other factors that helped propel the movement for cooperation were the information explosion, which made it difficult for libraries to keep up with the flood of books and journals being published, and the 1966 renewal of the Library Services and Construction Act, which added Title III, Interlibrary Cooperation. This new title specifically promoted multitype library cooperation and allowed libraries of all types to apply for this funding. A number of national networks quickly emerged.

We have already read about the establishment of the Ohio College Library Center (later the Online College Library Center) in 1967, which began using the MARC record to deliver catalog cards through automation. This system went online in 1971 and quickly became a national network. In addition to becoming a nationally shared cataloging system, OCLC branched into other areas, including a very successful interlibrary loan system. We have also already seen that the Research Libraries Group (RLG) was organized in 1974 to identify collections strengths and minimize duplication among these major research libraries: New York Public, Yale, Harvard, and Columbia. In 1979, they were joined by Stanford University, whose automated library system, called BALLOTS, was modified to become the Research Libraries Network (RLIN). Within the next three years, almost all of the large research libraries began to use the RLIN for shared cataloging.

Now let us take a close look at MILC, OCLC, and RLG in the pages that follow.

In the mid-1960s, MILC changed its focus from a regional, mid-western organization to one with a national scope, and changed its name in 1965 to the Center for Research Libraries. By 1967–1968, the center had 33 members; by 1973–1974 there were 130 members.

CRL today has almost 200 participating institutions and a collection of four million items, with emphasis on materials produced outside of the United States. As a consortium of North American universities, colleges, and independent research libraries, CRL acquires and preserves traditional and digital resources for research and teaching, and makes them available to member institutions through interlibrary loan and electronic delivery.

OCLC was established in 1967 under the direction of Frederick G. Kilgour in Columbus, Ohio, as the Ohio College Center for developing a computerized system in which Ohio academic libraries could share resources and reduce costs. It is now the OCLC Online Computer Library Center, Inc., providing computer-based cataloging, reference, resource sharing, e-content, and preservation services to 54,000 libraries in 109 countries.

OCLC's alliances with regional library networks in the 1970s were a major factor both in OCLC's rapid development and in rapid adoption of new OCLC services by the U.S. library community, as shown in table 3.1.

Table 3.1.   OCLC Alliances

1972	1974	1975	1976	1977
OCLC	FAUL	MLNC	BCR	PACNET
NELINET	FEDLINK	ILLINET	CAPCON	MINITEX
PRLC	AMIGOS	SOLINET	INCOLSA	NEBASE
	PALINET	SUNY	MLC	MRLN
			WiLS	

The above have now evolved to 16 regional services centers, as follows:

AMIGOS Library Services, Inc.—Serving southwest states

BCR—Bibliographic Center for Research serving Iowa and western states

ILLINET—Illinois Library and Information Network

INCOLSA—Indiana Cooperative Library Systems Services Authority
MINITEX—Minnesota Interlibrary Telecommunications Network
MLC—Michigan Library Consortium
MLNC—Missouri Library Network Corporation
NEBASE—Serving Nebraska
NELINET—New England Library Information Network
NYLINK—Serving New York State
OCLC CAPCON—Serving D.C., Maryland, and Virginia
OCLC Western Service Center
OHIONET—Serving Ohio
PALINET—Serving Pennsylvania, W. Virginia, and New Jersey
SOLINET—Southeastern Library Network
WiLS—Wisconsin Library Services

In addition, there are five global service providers: OCLC Canada, OCLC Latin American and the Caribbean, OCLC Middle East and Northern Africa, OCLC PICA (Europe and Southern Africa), and OCLC Asia Pacific.

OCLC will be celebrating forty years of progress and technological innovation in 2007. Here are some highlights of its history.

1968—MARC format developed at the Library of Congress
1969—Start of OCLC offline catalog card production
1971—Online shared cataloging system begins operation
1973—MIDO Beehive terminal becomes available
1974—CONSER begins building database of authoritative serial records (1.1 million records by 2005)
1974—WorldCat reaches 1 million bibliographic records
1975—OCLC Office of Research is established
1979—Interlibrary loan system becomes available
        First international member library (from Canada)
        OCLC libraries in all fifty states
1980—New OCLC building in Dublin, Ohio
1981—Acquisitions subsystem is added
        OCLC Europe is formed
1983—WorldCat totals 10 million bibliographic records

1988—Forest Press, publisher of the Dewey decimal classification, becomes part of OCLC

1990—EPIC service is introduced (subject access to WorldCat)

1991—FirstSearch is available

1993—Keyword searching

1995—WorldCat reaches 31 million records

Internet access to OCLC cataloging and resource sharing

1996—World Wide Web access to FirstSearch

1997—Electronic Collection makes journals available online

1998—Western library network merges with OCLC

1999—OCLC Cataloging Express for school and public libraries with low-volume cataloging

2000—OCLC Digital Archives launched

2002—Acquisition of NetLibrary, which emerges as leading provider of e-books for libraries

Gates Foundation provides $9 million for OCLC to build a Web-based, public access computing portal for 12,000 public libraries for training in technology

2004—Online Service Center is established

2005—61 million records in WorldCat

The Research Libraries Group was founded in 1974 by the New York Public Library and Columbia, Harvard, and Yale Universities. It is governed and administered by its members, staff, and board of directors. RLG now has over 150 worldwide members and supports researchers and learners by expanding access to research materials held in libraries, archives, and museums.

A chronology of major RLG developments is given below.

1978—RLG moves its offices to Stanford University. It adopts Stanford Library's BALLOTS computerized processing system, which will later become the Research Libraries Information Network (RLIN).

1980—A unique shared cataloging database—RLIN Union Catalog—is created

1983—RLG embarks upon several decade-long projects to preserve members' "Great Collections" on microfilm. Preservation microform information is included in online records for the first time.

1988—RLG moves to Mountain View, California

1989—100th member joins RLG

1990—RLG begins a decade-long series of member symposia focusing on the challenge of managing nonprint and electronic materials

1991—Ariel is introduced, a document transmission software for use in interlibrary transactions

1992—First member outside North America—the British Library
    Introduction of article-level access to journals and conference proceedings with the CitaDel citation databases

1993—Eureka is introduced, easy-to-use search system for non-librarians

1996—RLG opens its once-private network, allowing anyone in the world with Internet access to take advantage of RLG's services

2000—ILL Manager is introduced, a freestanding, easy-to-use software system for interlibrary loan transactions

2001—RLG receives a grant from the Andrew W. Mellon Foundation to create RedLightGreen, The RLG Union Catalog on the Web.

2002—New York City Office is opened

2004—CAMIO (Catalog of Art Museum Images Online) is created, taking the place of AMICO.

2005—Archives Grid is made available to the public, access to information stored in archives all over the world.

An examination of library cooperation in Buffalo and the surrounding western New York area in 1945 and 2005 proves most revealing. The 1945 *American Library Directory* and other sources show almost 100 academic, public, special, and school libraries (primarily high school) in 1945. There are no records of any library systems, consortia, or networks in the Buffalo area.

Current data from the 2005/2006 *American Library Directory* and the Western New York Library Resources Council (WNYLRC) show 612 libraries of all types—academic, public school, and special. In terms of cooperation, this six-county region has three public library systems and four school library systems. WNYLRC is a consortium of libraries and library systems serving six counties—one of nine such institutions in New York State. There are also 23 public library systems and 42 school library systems in New York.

In addition, individual libraries in Buffalo and western New York may be members of a wide range of other cooperative organizations such as NYLINK, the NYS Interlibrary Loan Network, the Library Consortium of Health Institutions in Buffalo, and the National Network of Libraries of Medicine.

> The same can be said on a national level, with a dramatic increase in library cooperation in the past forty years. All data is taken from the *American Library Directory* (ALD).
> The 1960 ALD volume lists 14 bibliographic centers.
> In 1974–1975, the ALD has its first list of library consortia—191 are described.
> The 1976–1977 volume of ALD has a broader listing entitled "Networks, Consortia and Other Cooperating Library Organizations"—345 are listed.
> The 2005/2006 ALD lists 401 consortia and 703 library systems.

And so we have seen the tremendous growth and impact of libraries joining into cooperative ventures to enhance access to information, encourage resource sharing, and promote library interests. Continuing education and research projects have also been among their important activities.

Those who were present in the profession in the 1950s and 1960s—before the advent of bibliographic utilities—can well remember large numbers of catalogers doing duplicative cataloging in each library. Another example was interlibrary loan, which first involved complex searches for verification of elusive citations followed by typing the ALA four-part ILL forms to be mailed to possible holding libraries, and then waiting for weeks or even months for a hopefully positive response.

Much of the progress in library cooperation would not have been possible without the support from the federal government, philanthropic organizations, and the Council on Library and Information Resources. A historical look at their activities and contributions is provided in the next chapter.

Federal Funding, Philanthropy, and the Council on Library and Information Resources

This chapter brings three related topics together—federal aid to libraries, library philanthropy, and the Council on Library and Information Resources. Federal funding had a major impact on library development and is covered in many appropriate parts of this work, but an overview is provided here.

Philanthropy has had a steadily growing impact on libraries during the past 50 years. And the Council on Library and Information Resources, itself a product of philanthropy, has been a major force in library development since the 1960s.

FEDERAL AID TO LIBRARIES

Detailed descriptions of federal funding are found in various sections of this study, but it is important to treat this as a general topic in order to focus on its importance in library development.

One of the greatest impacts on the growth of librarianship during the late 1950s and the 1960s was that of federal funding. ALA and librarians had been seeking federal funding since the 1930s. The pressure was intensified after World War II and was finally rewarded in 1956 with the passage of the Library Services Act, which authorized up to $7,500,000 yearly for the extension of library service to rural areas without such service or with inadequate services. LSA was a success and was extended by Congress in 1960 for five more years with overwhelming support.

There were other legislative acts passed that also had an indirect, positive impact on the development of libraries. Among these were the Presidential Libraries Act of 1955, the National Defense Act of 1958 (which provided for the purchase of a few selected areas of materials by school libraries), Public Law 480 in 1961 (which benefited over 300 academic libraries by allowing them to acquire and catalog copies of publications from eight countries through the expenditures of blocked currencies), the Depository Act of 1962 (which expanded the number of libraries that could become government document depositories), and the Academic Facilities Act of 1963 (which provided matching funds for the construction of library buildings to both public and private institutions).

On February 11, 1964, President Lyndon B. Johnson signed the Library Services and Construction Act. Unlike LSA, LSCA became a broad-based program of aid to all public libraries, urban as well as rural. Funds were also authorized for the first time for the construction and remodeling of libraries. A 1966 renewal of LSCA added Title III (Interlibrary Cooperation) and Title IV (Specialized State Services for Handicapped and Institutional Clients). By the end of 1972, more than 1,800 public library buildings (serving more than 60 million people) had been built or remodeled through LSCA funds and matching funds from state and local sources.

The Medical Library Assistance Act of 1965 provided funds for the construction of medical libraries, training of librarians, expansion of medical library resources, and the development of a national system of eleven regional health science libraries under the National Library of Medicine.

The Higher Education Act of 1965 provided three library programs: Title II-A, funds for acquisition of books, periodicals, and other materials for college and university libraries; Title II-B, library training and research/demonstration programs; and Title II-C, a centralized cataloging and acquisitions program under the direction of the Library of Congress.

Also, 1965 saw the passage of the Elementary and Secondary Education Act, which in Title II provided grants to states for the purchase of books, periodicals, and audiovisuals for public and private school libraries. The addition of school library supervisors at the state department of education level in a number of states was also made possible under this act.

All together, during 1964 and 1965, seven categorical aid programs had been enacted—two for public libraries, one for school libraries, three for college and university libraries, and one for medical libraries. There were, in addition, other acts that provided opportunities for libraries to receive funding during the 1960s. Among these were the Economic Opportunity Act, the Vocational Education Bill, the Appalachian Regional Development Act, and the National Foundation on the Arts and Humanities Act.

Finally, in 1966, President Johnson established the National Commission on Libraries, which recommended that it be declared national policy, enunciated by the president, and enacted by Congress, that the American people should be provided with library and information services adequate to their needs, and that the federal government, in collaboration with state and local governments and private agencies, should exercise leadership in assuming the provision of such services.

One of the commission's key recommendations was enacted with the passage of the National Commission on Libraries and Information Science (NCLIS) Act of 1970. This created a permanent, independent commission to analyze the country's library and information needs, appraise current resources and services, and develop overall plans for meeting national library and information needs and for the coordination of activities at the federal, state, and local levels. It was also to promote research and development activities that would extend and improve the nation's library and information handling capabilities.

Throughout the 1970s, 1980s, and 1990s, most presidents proposed reduced or no funding for library programs—inevitably overruled by Congress after intense lobbying by librarians.

In 1975, the National Commission on Library and Information Science published "Toward a National Program for Library and Information Science," which was an appeal to the federal government to subsidize the creation of a nationwide network of libraries and information centers and an integrated system encompassing state, multistate, and specialized networks in the public and private sector.

In 1979, the first White House Conference on Libraries was funded by the government. The conference convened in Washington, D.C., on

November 15, 1979, more than two decades after the idea was first proposed by Channing Bete, Sr. a library trustee from Greenfield, Massachusetts. There were five user-oriented themes: library and information
services for personal needs, lifelong learning, organizations and professions, governing society, and international cooperation and understanding. Among the conference speeches were those by Senator Javits
of New York, Governor Bill Clinton of Arkansas, and Ralph Nader.

A total of 64 resolutions were approved by 806 delegates and alternate
delegates chosen at the state level. Among the major goals were reshap-
ing library and information services in more useful ways, maintaining
local control of these services, and insisting on more economy and ac-
countability from the institutions that provide such services. One of the
64 resolutions passed called for a White House conference to be held
every decade. A task force was appointed to follow up on such actions.

In 1982, the U.S. Postal Service issued a commemorative first-class
postage stamp honoring America's libraries. In 2000, the Library of
Congress was honored by a U.S. stamp, as were presidential libraries
in 2005 on the 50th anniversary of the Presidential Libraries Act.

The 1991 White House Conference on Libraries had three goals: to
enhance literacy, to increase productivity, and to strengthen democracy.
The collected visions, ideas, and recommendations of the 900 delegates
yielded ninety-five recommendations in all, of which the following
were earmarked for priority:

- Adopt omnibus children and youth literacy initiative
- Share information via network "superhighway"
- Fund libraries sufficiently to aid U.S. productivity
- Create model library marketing programs
- Emphasize literacy initiatives to aid the disadvantaged
- Adopt national policies for information preservation
- Develop networking equity for low-density areas
- Encourage multicultural, multilingual program/staffs
- Amend copyright status for new technologies
- Ensure access to government information resources
- Enact national information policies for democracy
- Recognize libraries as partners in lifelong education
- Designate libraries as educational agencies

The year 1996 was a momentous one, with the reorganization of the federal agency administering library funding. Library programs were moved from the Department of Education to the new Institute of Museum and Library Service. The Library Services and Technology Act (replacing LSCA and some of the purposes of the former Higher Education Act Title II library programs) was passed with an increased focus on information access. Also in 1996, the Telecommunication Act provided equitable access to electronic information and recognized the role of libraries as crucial to that access through financial support.

The Institute of Museum and Library Services became the primary source of federal support for some 122,000 libraries and 15,000 museums. LSTA was designed to:

- Consolidate federal library service programs
- Stimulate excellence and promote access to learning and information resources in all types of libraries for individuals of all ages
- Promote library services that provide all users access to information through state, regional, national, and international electronic networks
- Provide linkages among and between libraries
- Promote targeted library services to people of diverse geographic, cultural, and socioeconomic backgrounds; to individuals with disabilities; and to people with limited functional literacy or information skills.

Federal funding for libraries began with $7,500,000 authorized under the Library Services Act of 1956. By the year 2005, $205,195,000 was available for all library services and technology programs.

LIBRARY PHILANTHROPY

The period of 1945–2005 was one of growing philanthropic contributions to libraries. Library data from the Foundation Center in New York City shows $33,308,912 provided to U.S. libraries during 1980–1981 from private foundations. By 2003, these contributions had grown to $165,759,000, though they had been as high as $271,557,000 in 2000 as reported by the same source.

The Carnegie Corporation continued its support of libraries through the 1950s. It made important contributions in its funding of the Public Library Inquiry in the late 1940s and in support of film library service in public libraries. With the advent of federal aid to libraries as well as other philanthropic library agencies, the Carnegie Corporation no longer had libraries as a high priority beginning with the 1960s.

Starting with 1947, the Great Books Foundation began to support free group discussions of "great" books in U.S. public libraries.

In the early 1950s, the Ford Foundation through the Fund for Adult Education provided ALA $1,394,000 for a number of key activities: the American Heritage Discussion Series, a survey of adult education activities in the United States, the Library Community Project, an Allerton Park Conference on the training needs of libraries doing adult education work, and various grants to individual libraries for adult education programs.

The Ford Foundation grant to establish the Council on Library Resources in 1956 was a major event. The important impact of the CLR grants on library development is explored in the last section of this chapter. Mention has already been made of the Knapp Foundation support for the Knapp School Libraries Project during 1968–1977.

The H. W. Wilson Foundation was established in 1952 by Halsey Wilson, founder of the H. W. Wilson Company. In 1957, the foundation gave its first grant to a library school for its scholarship program. Since then it has continued its role as a benefactor to library schools and also supports other library-related programs. Recent examples include the following:

1995—$50,000 to the Library of Congress Center for the Book to support "Shape Your Future—Read," the center's 1995–1996 national reading campaign

2000—$50,000 to a new building fund for the Graduate School of Library and Information Science at the University of Illinois

2003—$150,000 to the Reed College Library, a three-year grant for the purchase of electronic resources

2005—$50,000 to support the ALA Cultural Communities Fund to help libraries host arts and humanities programs in response to an NEH challenge grant

2006—$50,000 to ALA's Hurricane Katrina Library Relief Fund

The H. W. Wilson Foundation has supported accredited MLS programs in the United States and Canada with scholarship grants for many years.

Examples of library philanthropy in the United States are numerous and varied. In 1977, the university libraries at the University of Pittsburgh received $100,000 from the proceeds of the 1977 Sugar Bowl football game for library acquisitions. In the same year, Edmund and Louise Uraff Kahn made three $1 million gifts to the University of Pennsylvania Libraries (his alma mater), to the Smith College Library (her alma mater), and to the Dallas Public Library (their residence). In 1978, the Astor Foundation gave a $5 million challenge grant to the New York Public Library (NYPL) provided the library raised $10 million from other sources. In 1985, the Astor Foundation provided an additional $10 million to NYPL followed by a gift of $2.5 million from David Rockefeller in honor of Mrs. Astor. In 1982, the Xerox Corporation gave 200 Kurzweil reading machines (valued at $3 million) to selected U.S. college libraries. The Polaroid Corporation was not to be outdone: It donated 20,000 cameras to U.S. public libraries. In 1987, after his announcement of retirement as Librarian of Congress, Donald J. Boorstin revealed that he and his wife, as a token of love for the library and recognition of its role, were donating $100,000 to establish the Daniel J. and Ruth F. Boorstin Publication Fund.

During the past 15 years, we find more examples of library philanthropy. Kodansha International, one of Japan's leading publishers, awarded New York Public Library $1.3 million to expand its Oriental division and to increase access to its collection (1992). The Miller Brewing Co. donated $150,000 to finance Milwaukee Public Library's Read About Me Project (1993). During the mid-1990s, Ameritech, AT&T, Bell Atlantic, Kodak, and Reuters donated $9 million to the Library of Congress for its Digital Library Program. Jerry Jones, owner of the Dallas Cowboys, donated $1 million to replace books from the Thomas Jefferson Library that were lost in an 1851 fire that burned nearly two-thirds of the collection at the Library of Congress (1999). Thomas R. Drey Jr., a teacher, left his entire $6.8 million estate to the Kirstein Business Branch of Boston Public Library in Massachusetts (2000). An anonymous donation of $150,000 was given to Chatham-Effigham-Liberty Regional Library in Savannah, Georgia, to complete an addition to its "historically black Carnegie Library branch" (2001). A $1 million donation was provided to the Loudoun County (Virginia) Library to fund programs on Jewish culture (2001). The Wallace Foundation donated $2 million to each of three public library systems in New York City to improve programming for children (2004). An anonymous donation of $125,000 was given to the Bedford Public Library in Texas to keep the library from closing (2005). Oprah Winfrey's Angel Network Book Club donated $50,000 to ALA's Young Adult Library Services Association to support a national book club program targeting at-risk teens (2005).

All of the above gifts illustrate the wide variety of sources for library philanthropy as well as the many ways that libraries were helped. Many of the larger academic and public libraries have developed respectable endowment funds in support of collection development through the generous support of individual donors.

Indeed, since the mid-1980s, many larger public libraries and private research libraries have established their own library foundations as well as fund-raising staff. In 1987, Doral, NA was established—Development Officers of Research Academic Libraries, North America. In 1995, the Academic Library Advancement and Development Network (ALADN) was formed for professionals in academic library fund-raising. An annual conference, listserv, and personal contacts are available.

Fund-raising activity among all types and sizes of libraries has grown since the mid-1980s in reaction to less support from traditional sources. Evidence of this can be found in an increase in the number of library fund-raising books in the past 20 years. Also, the Foundation Center first began to publish separate data on foundation support to libraries in 1982.

ALA reflected these trends by establishing its own Development Office for Fundraising in 1990 and by the Campaign for American Libraries. The William K. Kellogg Foundation gave a two-year grant in 1995 to ALA to provide fund-raising training for library directors and board members in small to midsized public libraries.

As indicated earlier, after World War II, the Carnegie Corporation's support for individual public and academic libraries in the United States began to abate. More emphasis was placed on grants for central services provided by the American Library Association, the Association of Research Libraries, and the Library of Congress, and for new technologies and equipment to facilitate library use.

In 1986, on the 75th anniversary of the Carnegie Corporation, a $560,000 grant was provided through the ALA for videocassettes recorders to 600 of the 1,412 communities that had received grants for Carnegie Library buildings. In the spirit of the original Carnegie Library philanthropy, libraries were asked to match the VCR gift with either a television monitor or $300 in educational/cultural programming.

In recent years, the Carnegie Corporation has continued to make occasional gifts to libraries. In 1999, the corporation awarded $15 million to the New York Public Library, Brooklyn Public Library, Queens Borough Public Library, and libraries in 22 other cities serving large, culturally diverse populations. The grants marked the centennial period of Andrew Carnegie gifts to establish public libraries in New York City and more than 1,400 other communities across America. In 2000, in recognition of the great reach and service of the nation's rural and small libraries, a $1 million grant was made to the National Endowment for the Humanities, which in turn administered a competition to select approximately 800 small and rural libraries that would receive the most recent 50-volume collection of the Library of America Great Book series.

In 2002, in honor of the seven recipients of the first Andrew Carnegie Medals of Philanthropy, the corporation provided a $2 million grant to enhance the book collections in public libraries in which the honorees resided—Atlanta, Philadelphia, New York City, and Seattle. In 2003, the corporation made grants of $4.5 million to the three New York public library systems and $1 million to the District of Columbia College Access Program in memory of the men, women, and children killed in New York City and at the Pentagon on September 11, 2001.

But the biggest news recently in library philanthropy has been Bill Gates. Beginning in 1997, Microsoft chairman Bill Gates became a major benefactor of libraries through the establishment of the Bill and Melinda Gates Foundation. The largest gift to U.S. public libraries since Andrew Carnegie's, the Gates Program brought computer packages into the majority of public libraries in all 50 states by the end of 2003—40,000 computers in about 10,000 eligible facilities at a cost of $250 million.

The goal of the Gates Program was to bring access to computers, the Internet, and digital information to patrons in low-income and disadvantaged communities. Foundation trainees logged thousands of miles to install equipment and conduct hands-on training. Ongoing training has also been provided as well as funding for hardware upgrading. A 2004 survey sponsored by ALA and the Gates Foundation showed that 98.9% of public libraries offer free access to computers and the Internet. In 1996, just one in four libraries did.

A different source of philanthropy has come from the Friends of the Library groups found in many libraries. They often serve as fund-raising agents for the benefit of their library. In 1974, Friends of Libraries USA was established as a national association and now has over 2,000 individual and group member organizations.

Finally, the volunteers who often help staff libraries or work on library projects for no pay must be noted. Such volunteers can be characterized as still another form of library philanthropy. Public libraries in the United States in particular began to recruit and rely on volunteer help during the budget crises of the 1970s. Libraries continue to count on their assistance.

Foundation support for libraries was in the $20 million level in the mid-1970s. It is now around the $200 million level. Dramatic proof of how much libraries continue to rely on such support is in the latest edition of *The Big Book of Library Grant Money 2006*, prepared by Taft for the ALA. It is indeed a big book describing almost 2,400 philanthropic and corporate programs that are either active or potential supporters of libraries.

COUNCIL ON LIBRARY AND INFORMATION RESOURCES

The CLIR has been an important force in library development since its founding in 1956 with an initial Ford Foundation grant of $5,000,000. It was established for the purpose of aiding in the solution of the problems of libraries and of research libraries in particular through grants, research, the development and demonstration of new techniques and methods, and the dissemination of the results. As we shall see, CLIR has succeeded admirably in achieving its charge. The Council on Library Resources (CLR) became the Council on Library and Information Resources (CLIR) in 1997.

It was Louis B. Wright, director of the Folger Library in Washington, D.C., who almost single-handedly founded the Council on Library Resources. Wright was convinced that research libraries faced serious problems requiring help from a new kind of organization. Fortunately, he was a friend of Fred Cole, Ford Foundation Program Officer for Education, and persuaded Cole and the Ford Foundation Board of Trustees to provide support. Wright got some key research library leaders together to submit a grant request that was approved by the Ford Foundation. Verner Clapp, second in command at the Library of Congress, became the first president of CLR. This proved to be an excellent choice in the critical early years of the council.

What follows is a selected listing of CLR and later CLIR activities and contributions. In many cases, only a brief mention is made of some because they are explained in greater detail in other sections of this work. Some CLIR grants are described only in the sections on academic, public, and school libraries.

CLR began immediately to make important contributions to librarianship in a variety of ways. One was the publication of bibliographic tools of national significance, such as the third edition of the *Union List of Serials* (1965) and *The National Union Catalog of Manuscript Collections* (1962–1993). There was also financial assistance to ALA in 1961 to launch *Choice,* a monthly book-selection service for academic and public libraries, and in 1967 for the publication *Books for College Libraries.*

CLR made grants to ALA for the establishment of the Library Technology Project (LTP). Its purpose was to collect and disseminate to the library profession information and guidance concerning the use of modern techniques and machines in libraries. Besides listing products such as book trucks, shelving, and carpet underlay, LTP sponsored and guided the development of needed new equipment such as the Se-Lin labeling system for book spines. Eventually there were reports on automated systems and computer software. Reports of all testing programs were published in *Library Technology Reports,* which continues to this day as a valuable source.

Several seminal studies in the application of computer technology to bibliographic processes were undertaken in 1958 at the National Library of Medicine (NLM) and at the Library of Congress (throughout the 1960s). At NLM, this involved the mechanized production of its *Current List of Medical Literature,* which in 1960 became *Index Medicus* and was to eventually become *MEDLARS.* At the LC, studies eventually led toward automation of its system and the construction of an automated national database.

In 1968, with CLR assistance, the MARC pilot project was undertaken by the LC. MARC began to provide a standard method for the transmission of bibliographic data on magnetic tape. It was now possible to think in terms of the cooperative creation of a national database that could be shared by libraries across the United States.

Between 1967 and 1977, CLR made key grants to new, developing bibliographic utilities such as NELINET (New England Information Network), OCLC, BALLOTS, the Washington Library Network (WLN), and SOLINET.

CLR assumed the initial management and funding role in 1974 for the CONSER (Conversion of Serials) program to create a comprehensive bibliographic database of serials in machine-readable form. In 1978, the second edition of the *Anglo-American Cataloging Rules* was published with CLR support (as the first edition had been in 1967).

It was also in 1978 that CLR began the Bibliographic Service Development Program (BSDP), a multiyear program that attempted to improve bibliographic products, control costs of technical processes in individual libraries, and improve access to information by all users.

The remaining CLR contributions are grouped into two larger categories: those involved with professional advancement of individuals through fellowships, internships, leadership institutes, research support, and so forth, and those in the area of preservation of library materials.

In 1968, a CLR Fellowship Program was established, providing research support for librarians. This was followed ten years later by a Faculty/Librarian Cooperative Research Program. In 1974, an Academic Library Management Intern Program was also established. In 1992, the Association of College and Research Libraries "College Libraries Director Mentor Program" began with CLR support.

During the 1990s CLR was concerned about how best to prepare current and future leaders for a changing and increasingly technological society. In 1999, CLIR joined with others to establish the Frye Leadership Institute. This two-week residential program annually brings mid-level administrators, librarians, information technologists, and faculty members to Emory University's campus in Atlanta to consider the challenges emerging from information service trends in higher education and the ways to respond to them.

More recently, CLIR began offering postdoctoral fellowships for work within academic and research libraries that are collaborating in the program. The fellowships are awarded to individuals with PhD degrees in the humanities. New models of scholarship that apply digital technologies to research and teaching are being developed by teams of scholars, technologists, and librarians in a process that CLIR feels could be strengthened by recruiting new PhDs into library work.

CLR involvement with preservation is covered in depth in the section on preservation of library materials, but some highlights need to be mentioned here. CLR support for preservation started early in 1957 with a grant to William J. Barrow and the W. J. Barrow Laboratory that resulted in specifications for permanent and durable paper that became available on the market. The year 1986 marked the publication of *Brittle Books* by CLR and by its establishment of the Commission on Preservation and Access. In 1987, *Slow Fires: On the Preservation of the Human Record* was produced as a film showing the need for collection preservation. In 1997, the Commission on Preservation and Access was merged with CLR to become CLIR. In 1998, CLIR was instrumental in establishing the Digital Library Federation. CLIR has played a leading role during the past 20 years in bringing about an awareness of the preservation problem in American academic libraries and in bringing together all concerned parties to deal with the problem.

CLIR has indeed been a leading force in libraries and librarianship for almost 50 years. It has done an outstanding job, especially considering that it needs to find outside funding to continue operation. The Ford Foundation support was there only for CLIR to get established during the first twenty years. Because it has always had a small staff, it has been necessary for CLIR to find collaborators to develop new ideas, structures, and activities for the advancement of libraries, higher education, and learning. CLIR has been a remarkable catalyst and a great success.

We have seen in this chapter that federal support for libraries and the CLIR both had their origins in 1956. The Carnegie Corporation of New York was the only major library grant-giver in the 1940s and 1950s. During the past four decades, however, all three forces—federal aid, library philanthropy, and the CLIR—have played a key role in library development.

CHAPTER 5

Library Associations, Intellectual Freedom, and International Relations

This chapter begins with a historical overview of professional library associations with an emphasis on ALA. Professional associations have played a key role during the past 60 years. This is followed by a look at the concept and practice of intellectual freedom as it has progressed since 1945—primarily through the guidance of the ALA. Finally, a review of international relations between the United States and the rest of the library world is provided—again, primarily through professional associations.

LIBRARY PROFESSIONAL ASSOCIATIONS

Professional associations, and particularly the ALA, have played an important role in almost every phase and development of libraries and librarianship since WWII. There are currently some 152 library associations in the United States, with at least 230,000 members. Fifty-six of these are national associations (or international but based here and with U.S. members). Seven are regional associations. There are 50 state library associations plus another 35 state library associations limited to school library media members.

The growth of national associations since WWII has been phenomenal. There were eleven professional organizations in operation by 1942, shown in table 5.1 with the date of establishment.

Between 1947 and 1993, 45 new national library associations were established, out of the total of 55 currently in existence. Twenty-three were formed in the 1970s. A closer analysis of the 45 established since

Table 5.1.   Professional Library Organizations in 1942

American Library Association	1876
Medical Library Association	1898
American Association of Law Libraries	1906
Special Libraries Association	1909
Association for Library and Information Science Education	1915
Catholic Library Association	1921
Music Library Association	1931
Association of Research Libraries	1932
Theatre Library Association	1937
Library Public Relations Council	1939
Council of National Library and Information Associations	1942

World War II breaks down as follows: Twenty-four represent specialization by library or librarian, eight are religious, and ten are ethnic library associations. Two did not fit any of the above categories: Beta Phi Mu and the Library Cat Society. Beta Phi Mu, the library and information science honor society, is included because it has many characteristics of a national association, particularly in its chapter activities. The Library Cat Society's primary aim is the promotion of cats in libraries; it is the only association devoted to library residents. See table 5.2 for a list of these 45 organizations.

Looking at the regional associations, we see that three have been established since World War II (see table 5.3).

State library associations had been well established before World War II, with the exception of Nevada (1946) and Alaska (1960).

Most of the 34 states (plus the District of Columbia) with separate school library associations were established during the 1950s and 1960s but reorganized as educational media associations during the 1970s after merging with state audiovisual associations.

The great increase of specialized national associations from the 1940s to the 1970s was a result of the tremendous growth in libraries and librarians. The number of libraries more than tripled (from 31,000 in 1947 to an estimated 105,000 in 1970), while the number of librarians more than doubled (from 52,000 in 1950 to 120,000 in 1970). Another factor in the greater number of national associations was the increasing specialization of the field itself with the information explosion and the establishment of many specialized collections.

The stabilization in the growth of professional associations by the end of the 1980s can be explained by a number of factors. A slowdown

Table 5.2. List of Professional Library Associations since 1945

American Theological Library Association	1947
Beta Phi Mu International Library Science Honor Society	1948
Seminar on the Acquisition of Latin America Library Materials	1956
Association of Christian Librarians	1957
Council of Planning Librarians	1957
Lutheran Church Library Association	1958
Interagency Council on Library Resources for Nursing	1960
Ukrainian Library Association of America	1961
Association of Mental Health Librarians	1964
Association of Jewish Libraries*	1965
Church and Synagogue Library Association	1967
International Association of Orientalist Librarians	1967
Association for Population/Family Planning Libraries and Information Centers, International	1968
Association of Visual Science Librarians	1968
Black Caucus of the American Library Association	1970
Council on Botanical and Horticultural Libraries	1970
Evangelical Church Library Association	1970
International Council of Library Association Executives	1970
Polar Libraries Colloquy	1970
International Association of School Librarianship	1971
Reforma: National Association to Promote Library Services to the Spanish Speaking	1971
Urban Libraries Council	1971
Art Libraries Society of North America	1972
Council of Archives and Research Libraries in Jewish Studies	1972
Independent Research Libraries Association	1972
Middle East Librarians Association	1972
Chief Officers of State Library Agencies	1973
Chinese-American Librarians Association	1973
Association of Architectural Librarians	1974
Italian American Librarians Caucus	1974
Archivist and Librarians in the Health Sciences†	1975
International Association of Aquatic and Marine Science Libraries and Information Centers	1975
Jewish Librarians Task Force	1975
Association of Academic Health Sciences Library Directors	1978
Substance Abuse Librarians and Information Specialists	1978
Association of Architecture School Librarians	1979
American Indian Library Association	1979
Asian/Pacific American Librarians Association	1980
Online Audiovisual Catalogers	1980
Association of Seventh-Day Adventist Librarians	1981
Patent and Trademark Depository Library Association	1983
North American Serials Interest Groups	1984
Society of School Librarians International	1985
Library Cat Society	1987
African-American Library and Information Science Association	1993

*Merger of Jewish Librarians Association, 1962, and Jewish Library Association, 1946
†Formerly the Association of Librarians in the History of the Health Sciences

Table 5.3.   List of Professional Regional Associations

Pacific Northwest Library Association	1908
New England Educational Media Association	1918
Southeastern Library Association	1920
Mountain Plains Library Association	1948
New England Library Association	1963
Western Association of Map Librarians	1967

in the growth of libraries and librarians in the 1980s and 1990s was one cause, but perhaps the most important reason has been the Internet and other new sources for professional communication and interaction. Internet discussion lists are providing specialists and special-interest groups within our profession with a fast and effective way to exchange views and information that do not require an organizational umbrella.

ALA alone has more than 200 discussion lists available. Hundreds of others outside of ALA serve such specialized groups as library historians, doctoral students in library and information science, school library media specialists in Kentucky, Philadelphia-area law librarians, and so on.

Our professional associations are themselves becoming digital and virtual associations, particularly through their Web pages and use of the Internet for continuing education. It is truly a new era in professional association development.

The American Library Association is the oldest and largest of our professional associations and merits special attention. The Special Library Association was covered in the special libraries section and others are referred to wherever appropriate in the text.

The ALA has played a leading role in the development of libraries since 1945. Only highlights with emphasis on topics not covered elsewhere in this work are provided here. ALA activities involving federal aid, technology, intellectual freedom, library standards, accreditation, discrimination, diversity, and others are covered in the appropriate sections.

ALA development can certainly be measured in membership growth from 15,118 in 1945 to 64,000 in 2005. It can also be measured in space expansion—first, in the opening of an ALA Washington office in October 1945; second, when ALA moved to its own building in Chicago at 50 E. Huron (the old McCormick mansion) in 1946; and finally, with its move to a new building in Chicago planned for its own use in 1963, with an adjoining new building in 1981.

The celebration of ALA's 75th anniversary in 1951 was followed in 1955 by a management survey that resulted in a complete reorganizations of the association in 1957. There have been additional organizational changes down through the years, leading to the present structure of 11 divisions, each with many sections; 17 round tables; and a network of affiliates, chapters, and related organizations.

ALA has played a leading role in publicizing the importance of libraries through activities such as the establishment of National Library Week beginning in 1958, and through Library-21 at Century 21 at the Seattle World's Fair Exposition in 1962 and Library USA at the New York World's Fair during 1964 and 1965. Both of the latter provided a glimpse into the future of libraries and were seen by tens of thousands of visitors. National Legislative Day was established in 1973 and continues to this day. In 1981, ALA inaugurated its celebrity "Read" posters. The national library symbol adopted by ALA was approved for use by the Federal Highway Administration in 1985. Within the past few years, a public education initiative called "@ Your Library"—the campaign for America's libraries—was launched to speak loudly and clearly about the value of libraries and librarians in the twenty-first century.

The ALA conference of 1969 in Atlantic City was probably the most revolutionary library convention in library history anywhere. It led to the democratization of ALA and made it clear to the majority of membership that librarians were a part of society and that social issues were professional issues. Within the space of two years, the Social Responsibilities Round Table and the Black Caucus were established, as were the Task Force on Women and what is now called the Office for Literacy and Outreach Services. The ALA council ended the automatic membership of ALA past presidents, terminated all council terms at the end of 1972, and seated a new council at the January 1973 midwinter meeting.

The year 1972 saw the appointment of Robert Wedgeworth, an African American, as ALA executive director, replacing David Clift, who had served as executive director since 1951.

During the centennial of ALA in 1976, the first African American, Clara Stanton Jones, served as president. A book entitled *A History of the American Library Association, 1876–1972*, by Dennis Thomison, was published by the ALA in 1978. One other outcome of the centennial was that the ALA archives, which had been in disarray in an unheated Chicago warehouse, were then organized and cared for by the University of Illinois archives.

One of the greatest controversies within ALA occurred in 1977 when the Office for Intellectual Freedom received approval to develop a film on the First Amendment. *The Speaker* was a film about a high-school activities committee that decided to invite a controversial white speaker to present his opinions on the inferiority of the black race. It split the membership into dividing camps. Some clearly saw the film as racist; others disagreed. Many members who had struggled hard to bring about racial harmony and equality in the association felt betrayed.

In 1978, the ALA Association of College and Research Libraries held its own first conference, which then continued triennially and now biennially. A similar pattern followed with the first Association of School Librarians Conference in 1980 and the Public Library Association Conference in 1983.

Highlights from the past 20 years include the first female executive director, Linda Crisman, in 1987; the establishment of the ALA Literacy Assembly in 1989; the "Vision ALA Goal 2000—Intellectual Participation" adopted in 1995; the beginning of the Annual Congress on Professional Change in 1999; the @ Your Library campaign for America's libraries in 2001; the establishment of the ALA Allied Professional Association in 2002; and the adoption of a new strategic plan in 2005.

The @ Your Library program continues as a public awareness and advocacy campaign designed to showcase the value of public, school, academic, and special libraries and librarians in the twenty-first century. It was designed to remind the public that libraries are dynamic, modern community centers for learning, information, and entertainment.

The ALA–Allied Professional Association (ALA–APA) is a nonprofit organization chartered in Illinois and established "to promote the mutual professional interests of librarians and other library workers." ALA–APA is focused on two broad areas: the certification of individuals in specializations beyond the initial professional degree, and the direct support of comparable worth and pay equity initiatives, and other activities designed to improve the salaries and status of librarians and library workers.

By 2005, ALA developed a new strategic plan called "ALA Ahead to 2010," with six broad goals:

- Advocacy for libraries and the library profession
- The highest quality graduate and continuing education opportunities for librarians and library staff
- Formulation of national and international policies that affect library and information services
- Recruitment and development of a highly qualified and diverse work force
- Providing members with outstanding value for their ALA membership
- An inclusive, effectively governed, well-managed, and financially strong organization

DEFENSE OF INTELLECTUAL FREEDOM

The defense of intellectual freedom was one of the major accomplishments of librarianship during the past 60 years. The American Library Association was the key player in formulating a philosophy of and the structure for intellectual freedom. This historical overview covers the following aspects of intellectual freedom: against censorship of library materials, for free access to all to such material, protection of confidentiality of use of this material, the establishment of an administrative structure for intellectual freedom, and a review of recent events.

Against Censorship of Library Materials

ALA's opposition to censorship was present in 1939 due to pressures against John Steinbeck's *The Grapes of Wrath* being in library collections. Objections to this novel were based on the "immorality" of the book and/or opposition to the author's social views. The Library Bill of Rights was adopted in 1939 and listed the principles on which libraries opposed censorship and promoted intellectual freedom. In 1940, ALA established the Intellectual Freedom Committee (IFC) to recommend policies concerning intellectual freedom, especially involving violations of the Library Bill of Rights.

The original Library Bill of Rights focused on unbiased book selection, a balanced collection, and open meeting rooms. Since its adoption, there have been numerous revisions, amendments, and interpolations. Opposition to censorship of nonprint media was added to the document in 1951 because of attacks on films alleged to promote communism. A "statement on labeling" was added, which indicated that designating materials "subversive" was subtle censorship since a label predisposed readers against the materials. Because of pressures against materials in support of civil rights, a 1967 amendment to the Library Bill of Rights warned against exclusion of materials because of the author's social views.

Free Access

But opposition to censorship of library materials was not enough. Free access to every member of the community was another concern. A 1961 amendment to the Library Bill of Rights stated that "the rights of an individual to the use of a library should not be denied or abridged because of his race, religion, national origins, or political views." This was broadened in 1967 to include "social views" and "age." In 1980, another revision encompassed all discrimination of access based on "origin, age, background, or views." Various interpretations have been issued such as "Access for Children and Young People to Videotapes and Other Nonprint Formats," "Access to Resources and Services in the School Library Media Program," "Free Access to Libraries for Minors," "Economic Barriers to Information Access," and "Access to Library Resources and Services Regardless of Gender or Sexual Orientation."

Confidentiality

In 1970, U.S. government officials requested permission from a number of libraries to examine circulation records to find the names of persons reading materials about explosives and guerilla warfare. The ALA responded with a "Policy on Confidentiality of Library Records," urging libraries to designate such records as confidential and accessible only through a court order. In 1971, ALA asserted that the confidential relationship between librarians and people they serve should be respected in the same manner as medical doctors to their patients, lawyers to their clients, and clergy to the people they serve.

In 1987, it was discovered that FBI agents were visiting libraries in order to solicit information on the use of various library services such as circulation, interlibrary loan, and use of database searches by "suspicious looking foreigners" who might be foreign agents. The ALA confronted and challenged the FBI on this "Library Awareness Program," but the FBI refused to back down.

In the fall of 1989, through the Freedom of Information Act, the ALA obtained documents from the FBI on 266 individuals who had in some way criticized the Library Awareness Program and who were identified as subjects of FBI "index checks."

U.S. agencies were not the only ones attempting to get access to library patron records. Local law enforcement officials, journalists, parents, fund-raisers, marketing professionals, politicians, and others have and continue to seek borrowing records, registration data, mailing lists, and other information about registered library patrons.

Administrative Structure

In 1967, the Office for Intellectual Freedom (OIF) was established to conduct and coordinate ALA's intellectual freedom activities and to provide continuity for the total program, as well as to educate librarians and the general public on the importance of intellectual freedom and to serve as the administrative arm of the Intellectual Freedom Committee, which could now concentrate on formulating policy. The OIF began publishing a bimonthly newsletter and has produced numerous publications. The OIF also began advising and consulting with librarians confronting potential or actual censorship problems and coordinating with other organizations having similar concerns.

The concept of intellectual freedom also considered the individual librarian's intellectual freedom, both in pursuit of professional responsibilities and in personal life. In 1964, the Freedom to Read Foundation was established as an ALA response to librarians who needed a process to protect their jobs when they challenged violations of intellectual freedom. Another purpose for the foundation was a means through which librarians and others could begin to set legal precedents for the freedom to read. Although closely affiliated with ALA, the foundation was organized as legally and financially independent.

The LeRoy Merritt Humanitarian Fund was established by the Freedom to Read Foundation in 1970 in recognition of individuals' need for subsistence and other support when their positions were jeopardized or lost as a result of defending intellectual freedom. As an example, in 1979 Jeanne Layton, library director of Davis County, Utah, was dismissed from her position after she refused to remove a novel, *Americana,* by Don DeLitto, from the library shelves. The Intellectual Freedom Committee, the Office for Intellectual Freedom, and the Freedom to Read Foundation (with financial contributions) supported her suit to regain her job, which was successfully accomplished.

In 1973, the Intellectual Freedom Round Table (IFRT) was organized as ALA's membership activity program for intellectual freedom. The activities of this round table also supplemented the OIF's education program. The IFRT established three awards. First there was the John Phillip Immroth Memorial Award for Intellectual Freedom in 1975, given annually in memory of the cofounder and first chairperson of the round table "to honor notable contributions of personal courage in defense of freedom of expression." In 1984, IFRT began an annual State and Regional Achievement Award for a successful and creative intellectual freedom project, and biennially the IFRT sponsors the Eli M. Obler Award for the best published work in the area of intellectual freedom.

Recent Events

Since 1996 there have been a number of important developments. The Library Bill of Rights received three new interpretations: "Access to Electronic Information, Services and Networks" in 1996, "Intellectual Freedom Principles for Academic Libraries" in 2000, and "Privacy" in 2002.

In 1996, the Communications Decency Act (CDA) was signed into law by President Clinton to keep "indecent" material from anyone under 18 years of age. The provider of this material was subject to a fine up to $250,000 and/or up to two years in prison. Libraries and librarians were at risk because "indecent" was not defined. ALA filed a lawsuit challenging CDA's constitutionality. This suit was consolidated with and decided under a separate suit brought by the American Civil Liberties Union (ACLU). A lower court declared CDA unconstitutional and this was backed by a unanimous vote of the Supreme Court.

Congress then quickly passed the Child Online Protection Act (COPA) in 1998 to circumvent the Court's CDA decision, but was again rebuffed by the Courts.

The third attempt was the Children's Internet Protection Act (CIPA) in the year 2000. CIPA required libraries receiving certain federal funding to use technology that blocked or filtered material that was obscene, child pornography, or "harmful to minors" (when a minor was using the computer). Librarians were again placed in a difficult position. Furthermore, filtering was unreliable. In 2001, ALA and several allies filed suit challenging CIPA in the courts. Unfortunately, the Supreme Court ruled in June 2003 that CIPA was constitutional—thus challenging the library profession's core conviction—equal access to all. The other problem was the attachment of the filtered Internet access for adults, children, and library workers alike to the library acceptance of federal subsidies to defray communications expenses.

A more recent concern is the USA Patriot Act, passed hurriedly in the wake of the 9/11 attacks. This act allows liberal access to library records. Since its passage in 2001, ALA has been in the forefront of the battle to reform sections of the Patriot Act in order to restore privacy protection to the millions of Americans who rely on U.S. libraries. Most of the reforms sought by ALA were not included in the March 7, 2006, Patriot Act reauthorization bill passed by Congress and signed by the president.

The defense of intellectual freedom continues for the library profession. It remains one of our core beliefs. If we did not have the right to read, the freedom to learn, and the opportunities to be exposed to all varieties of ideas, then not many of the other accomplishments listed in this work would have been possible.

INTERNATIONAL RELATIONS

International relations for U.S. libraries were in effect during World War II in 1942 when ALA established the Board on International Relations.

An ALA International Relations Office was also established during the same year with a grant from the Rockefeller Foundation and space provided by the Library of Congress.

In a 1947 affirmation, ALA called for a better understanding of comparative librarianship, international cooperation, the development of exchange programs, and the exchange of information and ideas between the United States and other countries. An International Relations Round Table was established in 1948.

American libraries cooperated with UNESCO in its work with libraries throughout the world—particularly in helping libraries destroyed or damaged by WWII. ALA helped organize an American Book Center to coordinate efforts at restocking libraries in war areas of allied nations.

In 1957, the ALA International Relations Committee emphasized six fields of concentration: education of librarians, exchanges and observation abroad, building of collections, technical services, services to children, and publication.

In 1959, the ALA council adopted "Goals for Actions." Goal #5 called for increasing participation in the development of libraries and librarianship throughout the world through independent action and through cooperation with international organizations, such as the International Federation of Library Associations (IFLA). Indeed, the first postwar session of IFLA, Oslo 1947, was funded by a grant from the Rockefeller Foundation. An IFLA conference was held in Chicago in 1985 and in Boston in 2001. U.S. librarians have increasingly participated in IFLA, with Robert Wedgeworth serving as president.

ALA promoted international cooperation through its own conferences. In 1988, a delegation of Soviet librarians attended the annual conference and signed a protocol opening the way to the exchange of current national bibliographic data. In the same year, the ALA's International Relations Committee hosted the fourth binational U.S./Japan Conference on Library and Information Services in Higher Education. Also in 1988, ACRL held its first international meeting—a meeting of the Western European Specialists Section in Florence. It was also during 1988 when ALA began recruiting foreign librarians to attend the two conferences held each year. In 1997, ALA president Barbara Ford used "Global Reach/Local Touch" as the theme for her presidency.

During 1999, the American Association of School Librarians' (AASL) national conference was held in conjunction with the International Association of School Librarians in Birmingham, England.

Many other U.S. library associations welcome foreign members. Some based in the U.S. are international associations, such as the Beta Phi Mu International Library Science Honor Society, the International Association of Oriental Librarians, the International Council of Library Association Executives, the Polar Libraries Colloquy, the International Association of School Librarianship, the International Association of Aquatic and Marine Science Libraries and Information Centers, and the North American Serials Interest Group.

Joint cooperation has been evident between the United States, Canada, and Great Britain. ALA and CLA (Canadian Library Association) held joint conferences in Montreal in 1960 and in Toronto in 2003. In 1967, in 1977–1978, and in 1984, there was cooperation on the continued maintenance of the *Anglo-American Cataloging Rules* and the publication of AACR and AACR2 between the United States, Canada, and the United Kingdom.

The U.S. government has also played a major role. As an example, the Library of Congress National Program for Acquisitions and Cataloging assisted regions of the world in achieving bibliographic control over published items. At one time, there were thirteen centers across the globe, including Cairo, Jakarta, Karachi, Nairobi, New Delhi, Rio De Janeiro, and Moscow. The other major outreach activity of the federal government on behalf of libraries had been the overseas libraries of the United States Information Agency (USIA). Its libraries have served to demonstrate excellent public library service at sites across the world. At one time, there were 426 of these libraries and reading rooms, but these have now been greatly diminished in number.

OCLC has had a wide international impact. The use of OCLC abroad grew rapidly, first in the Netherlands in 1978, then to the United Kingdom in 1979, and on to continental Europe and the rest of the world. OCLC provides services to 54,000 libraries in 109 countries and territories. We have already seen international impacts of SPARC, JSTOR, and SLA.

Mention also needs to be made about exchange programs. The Fulbright Program has provided numerous opportunities for exchange of library scholars. Many schools of LIS have supported international students to obtain their MLS or PhD in the United States. The University of Pittsburgh has been a leader in this respect. The University at Buffalo hosted four faculty members at four different times from the Department of Library and Information Science at the Jagiellonian University in Krakow, Poland. From 1986 through 1998, the ALA Library Book Fellowship program, with a grant from USIA, made it possible for some 100 U.S. librarians to participate in exchange programs with 70 countries.

During 2004 and 2005, ALA's International Relations Office and International Relations Round Table provided leadership for assistance to libraries in Iraq and to those in Africa and Asia devastated by earthquakes and the tsunami.

Finally, it should be noted that U.S. library education programs have increasingly attracted and recruited international students. During 2003–2004, there were 516 MLS and 316 doctoral students enrolled from 104 countries.

Just as our economy has become global, so U.S. librarianship has become interconnected throughout the world. In this chapter, we have seen how U.S. professional library associations have grown and become more specialized and how they have made an impact in the development of the concepts and practices of intellectual freedom and in growing contacts with out international colleagues. We will continue to see their impact, and particularly that of ALA, in the forthcoming chapters.

CHAPTER 6

Gender and Ethnicity

This chapter traces diversity in the library profession. For many years, women were greatly underrepresented in library director positions of the larger libraries and not equitably paid in comparison to men. Since the 1970s, there have been improvements in both areas. As the post–World War II period began, some minority users had to use segregated libraries or had no access to libraries. Minority librarians were few in number and faced discrimination in professional associations and in their work. Great progress has been made, though more is necessary in the future. The rising tide of immigration after World War II and, in recent years, resulted in ethnic professional associations and special services to these groups in libraries.

WOMEN IN LIBRARIANSHIP

The percentage of women in the library profession has not changed dramatically during the period of this study. The census showed 88.8% female in 1950 and 82.6% female in 2000. What has changed is the positive increase in the number of women in the top library administrative positions, which had previously been the preserve of men.

Betty Friedan started this change with the publication of her book *The Feminine Mystique* in 1963. This marked the rebirth of feminism—often called the "second wave," with the first beginning in the nineteenth century. The National Organization for Women (NOW) was formed in 1966. This movement took action to bring women into full participation in the mainstream of American society. The aim was to eliminate discrimination in employment, job promotion, compensation, and in higher education admissions and athletics. Studies showed the disproportionate number of women in leadership positions, such as superintendent, principal, and library director.

This movement hit librarianship by 1970 with the establishment of the ALA Task Force on the Status of Women. Anita Schiller's study showing that women represented only 8% of academic library directors was also published at this time. The Women Library Workers was formed in 1976 as was the ALA Committee on the Status of Women. From 1974 to 1982, there was a boycott against holding ALA conferences in those states that had failed to ratify the Equal Rights Amendments.

From the late 1970s and into the 1990s, there was a flurry of books, articles, special issues of journals, speakers, and conference programs analyzing the role of women in librarianship. Women's library history also flourished. Affirmative action and pay equity were major issues.

In 1979, Kathleen Weibel and Kathleen M. Heim published a groundbreaking book entitled *The Role of Women in Librarianship, 1876–1976: The Entry, Advancement and Struggle for Equalization in One Profession.* This important work included an anthology of 44 selections, along with a bibliography of over 1,000 items arranged chronologically. This annotated bibliography has been updated in five-year supplements, each entitled *An Account of Sex: An Annotated Bibliography on the Status of Women in Librarianship.*

In 1984, the annual ALA Equity Award was established and given to an individual or group for outstanding contribution towards equality in the library profession. The award is given for an activist or scholarly contribution in such areas as pay equity, affirmative action, legislative work, and nonsexist education.

By the turn of the century, progress was in evidence:

- There was a shift in the number of female ALA presidents. From 1945 through 1974, the ratio was 20 men to 10 women. From 1975 through the president-elect for 2007, the ratio has almost reversed to 21 women to 11 men.
- Annual statistical reports from the Association for Library and Information Science Education show that in 1981, 41.7% of the LIS

faculty in accredited MLS programs were women. The latest report for 2004 shows that 50.7% are women.

- For deans/directors, there has also been progress, with 19% women in 1981 and 41% women in 2004. However, the 2004 data shows that the average salary for female deans/directors was $101,646 while that for men was $130,646. In 1981, the comparative figures were $37,622 for women and $43,799 for men.
- There were 27 female assistant professors appointed during 2003–2004 at an average salary of $53,522, while the 17 new male assistant professors received an average annual salary of $64,828.
- The Association of Research Libraries annual statistical compilations showed 75 male and nine female library directors during 1976–1977. The latest data for 2004–2005 shows 52 male and 60 female directors. The average salaries for the directors were $161,370 for males and $157,630 for women. The average salaries for professional staff in ARL libraries were $62,000 for men and $58,770 for women.
- Finally, the latest available data on placement of recent MLS graduates, compiled annually by the *Library Journal,* showed that the average beginning male salary was $40,332 and for women $38,704 during 2004.

And so for women there has been a better representation in key positions for the profession during the past 60 years but much remains to be accomplished—particularly in pay equity.

BLACK LIBRARIANS

The ALA as well as the other national library associations established before World War II were open to blacks, unlike most of the other national professional associations, which were open only to whites and often had parallel associations for blacks. However, the southern state library associations were segregated. ALA has fought racial discrimination within its own ranks and within librarianship on a number of fronts.

In 1948, the ALA Planning Committee issued *A National Plan for Public Library Service.* This plan identified lack of service to

African Americans as one of the most serious issues facing the library profession.

Plans to hold the 1954 annual conference in Miami Beach were abandoned when that city was not able to meet ALA's nondiscriminatory requirements. However, their requirements were met for the 1956 conference in Miami.

In 1954, ALA approved the idea of a single library association open to all in each state, thus forecasting the integration of state library associations. By 1964, the four remaining Southern state library associations were integrated.

In 1961, ALA amended the Library Bill of Rights so that the individual's right to use the library would not be denied or abridged because of race, religion, national origin, or political views.

In 1963, ALA published *Access to Public Libraries,* which identified two types of discrimination found in libraries. Direct discrimination (found in 16 Southern states) was complete exclusion of one racial group from using the library resources. Indirect discrimination was found throughout the United States. It referred to inequitable locations of library branches and unfair distribution of resources in these branches in terms of quantity and quality. The study provoked much controversy and protest, particularly over the methodology that was used for the libraries outside of the South, but was later proven to be basically factual and largely valid.

The following examples show the struggle to open libraries in the South to black citizens.

1962—In response to a number of library sit-ins, the Carnegie Library in Albany, Georgia, closes in August, but opens to blacks for the first time in March 1963 after 1,600 whites sign a petition asking the library to integrate its services.

1963—While trying to apply for library cards September 15 at the all-white public library in Anniston, Alabama, two young ministers are attacked by an angry mob.

1964—Twenty-five Freedom Libraries are established throughout Mississippi by a group of librarian volunteers in the civil rights movement.

1966—In *Brown v. Louisiana,* the U.S. Supreme Court rules that five African American demonstrators arrested during a 1964 sit-in at the Audubon Regional Library in Clinton, Louisiana, should not be charged with disturbing the peace. It is the only library segregation case to be argued in the U.S. Supreme Court.

The civil rights movement in the 1960s also started an explosion of books by and about black people, fostering a modern-day renaissance of African American literature. There were also new black publishers, black bookstores, and African American collections in public, academic, and school libraries. Many academic institutions inaugurated African American studies programs, which generated research and scholarly publications. The libraries of these institutions responded by developing collections to support the students and faculty of these programs.

Among public libraries, the following serve as examples of such collections:

1994—The Auburn Avenue Research Library on African American Culture and History opens as a special branch of the Atlanta-Fulton County Public Library System.

1999—The Vivian G. Harsh Research Collection of Afro-American History and Literature, the largest collection of its kind in the Midwest, opens as an expanded wing of Chicago Public Library's Woodson Regional Library.

2002—The African American Research Library and Cultural Center opens as a branch of Broward County Libraries in Fort Lauderdale, Florida.

2003—The Blair-Caldwell African American Research Library opens as part of the Denver Public Library system.

E. J. Josey's *Black Librarian in America,* published in 1970, was a seminal work and launched the modern period of African American librarianship. Josey founded the Black Caucus of ALA. He also edited the important *Handbook of Black Librarianship* in 1977. A second edition published in 2000 shows the progress that has been made, particularly through affirmative policies and procedures and the availability of hundreds of federal fellowships from the late 1960s into the early 1990s to recruit minorities at the MLS and doctoral levels. Josey was a prominent academic librarian and library educator who served as ALA president and continues as an activist and writer.

Robert Wedgeworth became the first African American executive director of ALA in 1972. In 1984, he became dean of the School of Library Service at Columbia University and later director of libraries at the University of Illinois and president of the International Federation of Library Associations.

In 1976, Clara S. Jones, who was the first black and first female director of the Detroit Public Library, was elected as the first African American president of ALA.

Vivian Davidson Hewitt served as the first black president of the Special Libraries Association in 1978.

We have already read about ALA's release of the film entitled *The Speaker*, which was a setback to many black librarians who felt that it had violated the ALA's Library Bill of Rights and was an affront to black people.

In 1982, New York State Senator Major R. Owens was the first librarian elected to the U.S. House of Representatives, where he serves to this date as a spokesman not only for his constituents but also for libraries and for African Americans.

Josey lists the activities and contributions of black librarians at the turn of the century. Among these were four directors of major public libraries, three LIS school deans, three directors of major research libraries, and one state library director. Dozens of others held prominent positions throughout the profession.

LIBRARIANS OF OTHER ETHNIC GROUPS

During 1971, REFORMA: The National Association to Promote Library and Information Services to Latinos and the Spanish-Speaking was established. There are currently twenty chapters throughout the United States, where it is estimated 56.2 million Spanish-speaking and Latino people reside. The goals of REFORMA include:

- Development of Spanish-language and Latino-oriented library collections
- Recruitment of bilingual, multicultural library personnel
- Promotion of public awareness of libraries and librarianship among Latinos
- Advocacy on behalf of the information needs of the Latino community
- Liaison to other professional organizations

Diverse ethnicity continued to express itself in the following years with the establishment of the Middle East Librarians Association in 1972, the Chinese American Librarians Association in 1973, the Italian American Librarian Caucus in 1974, the Jewish Librarians Task Force in 1973, the American Indian Association in 1979, and the Asian/ Pacific American Librarians Association in 1980.

By the 1990s, the foreign-born population of the United States had shifted from European countries to Mexico, Philippines, China and Hong Kong, India, Cuba, Vietnam, and Central American countries. The urban public libraries had always responded to immigration shifts and did so again to these new immigrants. The Queens Public Library is a prime example of such service, with collections in 80 languages and with services and programs for such diverse users. Library outreach to Spanish-speaking users has been especially growing in many parts of the United States.

Here is a representative listing of ALA groups working toward diversity in our profession:

- African American Studies Librarians Section, ALA Association of College and Research Libraries.
- Asian, African, and Middle Eastern Section, ALA Association of College and Research Libraries
- Committee on Cataloging Asian and African Materials, ALA Association for Library Collections and Technical Services
- Ethnic and Multicultural Information Exchange Round Table, American Library Association
- Instruction for Diverse Populations Committee, ALA Association of College and Research Libraries, Instruction Section

- Libraries Serving Special Populations Section, ALA Association of Specialized and Cooperative Library Agencies
- Library Services to the Spanish-Speaking Committee, ALA Reference and User Services Association, Management and Operation User Services Section
- Services to Multicultural Populations Committee, ALA Public Library Association

FUTURE DIVERSITY

The need to recruit and retain a diverse workforce has come to be seen as one of the crucial issues facing the library profession. If libraries are to become welcoming institutions to all, regardless of race and ethnicity, librarians and other workers must become more diverse.

In 1997, ALA approved the Spectrum Initiative, a recruitment and scholarship plan over a three- and later four-year period providing 50 $5,000 scholarships to students from underrepresented groups for MLS study. This program was extended and continues to this date with support from many library constituencies. This has now become ALA's national diversity effort designed to address the specific issue of underrepresentation of critically needed ethnic librarians. Spectrum's major drive is to recruit applicants and award scholarships to American Indian/Alaskan native, Asian, Black/African American, Hispanic/Latino, or Native Hawaiian/other Pacific Islander students.

In 1999, the ALA Office for Diversity was established to administer the Spectrum Initiative, to improve library service through a more ethnically diverse work force, and to serve as a key link and resource for diversity issues and actions of ALA.

The 1950 U.S. Census data showed 57,670 librarians, with 96.5% white, 3.1% black, and .4% other. The 2000 Census counted 190,255 librarians, with 86% white, 6% black, 3.3% Hispanic, 3.6% Asian, and 1.1% other. Hopefully, the next census will show continuing growth in diversity.

CHAPTER 7

Library Buildings and Preservation

Bringing together the two topics of library buildings and preservation may seem inappropriate at first, but they are connected. Library buildings are there to house and protect library collections. Recent developments in preservation have concentrated on safeguarding and preserving the human record from self-destruction. There has been an explosion of new library buildings since World War II that continues to this day. There has also been an explosion of preservation activity, especially since the late 1960s.

LIBRARY BUILDINGS

Without question, there was no other period of American library history that saw as much library building activity as 1945–1970—not even the Carnegie Library period of 1898–1917, when almost 2,000 public and academic library buildings were built. Indeed, many of those earlier Carnegie buildings were replaced or expanded.

Statistics for academic libraries are incomplete, but some examples will show the case. Between 1948 and 1957, 236 new academic library buildings were built. During 1961–1965, there were 504 new academic library buildings, while between 1966 and 1970, 258 new libraries were constructed on academic campuses.

The data is more complete for public libraries, as seen in table 7.1.

Libraries were leaders in the new American architecture that emerged around 1950. Architectural journals began to feature new libraries. The new buildings were, for the most part, modular, providing

Table 7.1.   New Library Construction, 1941–1970

1941–1950	733 (most after 1945)
1951–1960	1,140
1961–1970	3,364

flexibility in use. Air conditioning, fluorescent lighting, carpeting, group study rooms, and browsable, open-access shelving were features that made all library buildings more welcoming and human. Dozens of manufacturers began to produce library furniture and equipment.

Although the tempo lessened, library buildings continued to be built after 1970. There were 611 new academic library buildings built between 1972 and 2005. New public library building continued, as shown in table 7.2.

Table 7.2.   New Library Construction, 1972–2005

1971–1980	1,348
1981–1990	876
1991–2000	1,024
2001–2005	374

During the period 1968–2001, there were also 3,466 public libraries that had additions and major renovations. All of the above data comes from the *Bowker Annuals* during this period.

During the 1990s, library designers began to shift their focus. The design emphasis was now on people rather than shelving and other inanimate objects. Library interiors began to emphasize visible and attractive service points, comfortable seating, simplified pathways, and good signage. The open atrium became a popular feature, with service areas grouped around the open space. Another 1990s trend among larger academic libraries and some large public libraries was to place low-use materials in off-site storage. Successful public libraries began to turn their buildings into cultural community centers for their service areas. Academic libraries have started becoming academic or learning commons for their institutions of higher education. In recent years, some libraries have provided coffee and snacks in a comfortable seating area.

A decline in constructing new library buildings during the past fifteen years would have been a logical anticipation. Some have declared that technology is making the need for library buildings questionable, that print is obsolete, or that users can go online for information from their homes or offices. However, society seems unconvinced by the "library without walls" concept since many new buildings—some of them massive—have been built and are being planned in the United States and, indeed, throughout the world. The library building is still viewed as a preserver of accumulated knowledge, as a social and cultural institution, and as a place for librarians to do their work—particularly in personally interacting with users. Information technology does not replace face-to-face instruction or counseling; it merely facilitates these human interactions.

The yearly December 1 issues of the *Library Journal* provide dramatic evidence of new, often magnificent library buildings being constructed all over the country. Among the most recent and noteworthy have been large public library buildings in Chicago, Phoenix, Denver, San Antonio, Nashville, Seattle, and in San Francisco. Recent examples of major academic library buildings may be found at the University of Minnesota, the University of Washington, and the new undergraduate library at the University of North Carolina, Chapel Hill.

PRESERVATION OF LIBRARY MATERIALS

Preservation began to be formalized as a library function in the late 1960s and early 1970s. Preservation activities were developed to ensure the usability, longevity, and accessibility of recorded knowledge. Specific preservation activities included:

- Conservation: general collection repair, binding, and bringing items together in a special collection for special care
- Reformatting of endangered materials: through photocopying, deacidification, microfilming, and digitization
- Environmental monitoring and control
- Disaster preparedness and recovery
- Training in preservation

By the late 1960s, major collection problems became evident as a result of the paper-making begun in the nineteenth century. The use of acid in the paper-making process reduced costs but over time the residual acid slowly destroyed the paper, making it brittle. The Florence flood of 1966, which caused the loss of many irreplaceable cultural treasures, brought the realization that libraries could also lose their embrittled collections.

There had been earlier attempts to deacidify the acid paper, but the methods were costly and could not scale up to meet the problems of mass deacidification required by large collections of research libraries.

Although George Cunha established a conservation lab at the Boston Athenaeum in 1963, most of the activity began some six years later. In 1969, the Library of Congress established first the post of Restoration Officer and then a Conservation Department that offered apprenticeships for future conservators. Preservation units were also introduced at Yale University and the New York Public Library in 1972.

The American Library Association established a Committee on Preservation of Library Materials in 1970. A section on preservation was later created within the Association for Library Collections and Technical Services.

During 1973, Columbia University established the position of preservation librarian. In the same year, the New England Library Association created the New England Document Conservation Center, with George Cunha as head. Training workshops were also provided by the center.

In 1974, a formal conservation and preservation program was established at the Newberry Library in Chicago, with Paul Banks as director. Summer training workshops were also provided.

In 1975, Johns Hopkins University started a five-year conservation apprentice program. About the same time, a Conservation and Book Program was also established at the University of Iowa.

Paul Banks left the Newberry Library for Columbia University to teach conservation and direct conservation treatment of the university library collection. By 1981, a formal curriculum and degree program in preservation within the MLS was offered at Columbia. When the School of Library Service was closed down at Columbia in 1992, the preservation training program was transferred to the University of Texas, which had established a Conservation Department in 1980 and also offered training and apprenticeships to librarians.

The Council on Library Resources began playing a major role in preservation with the publication of *Brittle Books* in 1986. CLR also established a Commission on Preservation and Access in the same year. This became a separate but affiliated organization in 1988. In 1987, CLR was one of the sponsors of *Slow Fires: On the Preservation of the Human Record,* a film that was widely distributed and dramatically showed the need for collection preservation measures.

In the 1980s, the National Endowment for the Humanities (NEH) launched a nationally coordinated program to preserve the intellectual content of U.S. newspapers and brittle books through preservation microfilming. Supporting NEH and exerting national preservation leadership were such organizations as the Association of Research Libraries, the American Library Association, the Commission on Preservation and Access, the Library of Congress, and the Council on Library Resources. They led an advocacy campaign to promote preservation awareness through measures such as the adoption of acid-free paper by the publishing industry and an annual gathering of preservation statistics. By the early 1990s, most academic libraries had established distinct preservation programs.

March 7, 1989, was an important day in preservation history. Forty publishers agreed to use acid-free paper for all first printings of quality hardcover trade books. The American Library Association continued its concerns and activities by formulating a Preservation Policy in 1991. This was renewed in 2001 to take into account the preservation of digital information.

By the turn of the century, the library community, faced with new possibilities created by digital technology, realized that deacidification and digitization were important approaches to consider in addition to microfilming brittle books, especially with much improved methods in deacidification.

In 1997, the Commission on Preservation and Access merged with CLR, which was now renamed the Council on Library and Information Resources (CLIR). During 1997–1998 CLIR formed the Digital Library Federation, which eventually included over thirty organizations and became a leading force in digital library development.

As the digital revolution took hold, there was a realization among research libraries that a different preservation process was needed. Unlike print-based materials, which could be assessed for preservation years after their creation, digital materials that are worth preserving in accessible formats had to be designated for preservation at the time of their creation. Along with digital information, relatively new media such as film, television, and sound recordings were more fragile and more dependent on technology for transmission. Their preservation required more involvement by creators and administrators as well as librarians.

Also by the turn of the century, the microfilming of brittle books had declined and the number of preservation staff had dropped. The Brittle Books Program, which provided the focal point for a national preservation agenda during the 1980s and 1990s, had lost its momentum.

Preservation training had also decreased. During the late 1980s and early 1990s, there had been a proliferation of preservation courses in library schools as well as federal and state funded programs that helped to fill shortages of trained preservation librarians. By the mid and late 1990s, the array of preservation classes was decreased by the growing emphasis on computer technology and the closing of some schools. However, other venues like certificate programs, internships, workshops, and apprenticeships were still available.

Preservation in libraries received wide publicity beyond the profession in 2000 and 2001. Nicholson Baker, a well-known novelist and essayist, first wrote an essay entitled "Deadline: The Author's Bid to Save America's Past" in the July 24, 2000, issue of the *New Yorker.* He criticized librarians for destroying newspapers and depending on unreadable microfilm copies. Baker was convinced that lack of space—not paper deterioration—was the rationale for microfilming.

He enlarged the attack in *Double Fold: Libraries and the Assault on Paper,* published in 2001. In it, he accused librarians of no longer caring about their important role as custodians of civilization but instead to succumbing to trendiness and electronic glitz. In his book, he reviewed the activities underway in the reformatting through microfilming or digitizing of books and newspapers determined to be in dangerous condition. He believed that the supposed brittle nature of books and newspapers had been overblown. He argued that the cost of reformatting was far more than what it would be to store originals, and that the replacement of originals with surrogates undermined the scholarly use of books and journals.

Baker believed that everything should be saved, and that paper was the superior means of preserving information. He felt that librarians were stupid, misguided, or evil. He was particularly critical of the Council on Library and Information Resources for their preservation activities.

Libraries responded widely both in print and on the Web. They were outraged by purposeful misrepresentation and exaggeration, and angered by attacks on colleagues and their institutions. "Libraries are not museums" was another response.

One of the best responses came in a letter dated April 25, 2001, sent to the *New York Review of Books,* in which a favorable review of *Double Fold* had appeared. It was from Shirley K. Baker, president of the Association of Research Libraries. The last two paragraphs from the letter are shown below.

Research libraries in North America have almost 500 million print volumes in their collections and add another 10 million volumes each year. In a recent year, they spent over $83 million on a wide range of preservation strategies. Almost 3.5 million volumes were bound, 1 million volumes were restored through conservation treatment, 115,000 items were deacidified, and 156,000 items were placed in protective enclosures. In addition, 110,000 volumes were reformatted through microfilming or photocopying. Almost 50% of ARL's 122 member libraries report significant improvements in environmental conditions in their buildings over the past three years—controlled temperature and humidity being one of the most effective ways to prolong the life of library resources. Could libraries do more to preserve original artifacts? Of course, with additional funding, more materials could be preserved. Will this happen? Only with greater public commitment to preservation of the historical record.

Both Baker's book and Darnton's review have served to bring the preservation of print artifacts to the attention of the public. We hope that the interest generated will result in heightened visibility for the many successes that libraries have had in preserving our culture and a better understanding of the complex challenges that libraries face in acquiring, providing access to, and preserving materials in ever more numerous formats, with limited resources. We are glad to see the interest people have in this issue and hope that public discussion will elevate the importance of preservation and reaffirm the positive role research libraries play in this effort.

In 2002, CLIR, ARL, and others with federal funding conducted a study to examine the state of preservation programs in the U.S. academic libraries. This was published in 2002 by CLIR as *The State of Preservation Program in American College and Research Libraries: Building a Common Understanding and Action Agenda,* by Anne R. Kenney and Deidre C. Stam. The report recommended such areas of action as follows:

1. Encourage a common and more inclusive understanding of preservation to support program development.
2. Focus attention on pragmatic and measurable approaches.
3. Tailor knowledge and techniques to targeted audiences.
4. Address the digital preservation challenge at the local level.
5. Explore collaborative solutions that demonstrably benefit the home front.
6. Secure sustainable funding for preservation.

It was found that preservation as a core activity of librarians remained less visible than other areas, such as cataloging and user surveys. Libraries were working to integrate access to print materials with access to digital materials, and there is a challenge to integrate the preservation of analog and digital materials.

Preservation progress continues. On November 16, 2004, National Endowment for the Humanities chairman Bruce Cole announced the launching of a new effort—the National Digital Newspaper Program with the Library of Congress. Over 67 million pages of newspaper had already been microfilmed. The project is digitizing 30 million pages of U.S. newspapers, covering 1836–1922. The technique being used is OCR, Optical Character Recognition. On a computer screen, a whole page is shown with a zoom device that can focus on a single story. Keyword searching is available. All of this is a quantum leap from reading microfilm.

It is appropriate also to think about the preservation of the Internet. The Internet Archive Project (www.archive.org) is trying to preserve the look and feel of websites from the past. These "old" Web pages are rare in their own way. What about the preservation and documentation of this past? Writers who prepared an article in the year 2002 may have used websites in their research, properly including references to those websites in their footnotes and bibliographies—but four years later, these sites may have been changed or may not even exist.

The digital revolution has provided almost unlimited possibilities for wide dissemination of information and documents. Text can be scanned, placed on the Web, and made accessible anywhere in the world. But there are serious concerns about the long-term preservation of electronic information. Computer files less than a decade old may be difficult or even impossible to peruse because of lack of compatible hardware or software.

Most current books and microfilm preservation should be useable at least 500 years in the future. Most computer disks have a life expectancy of about five years. An extension to fifty years would still create problems of access to the hardware and software necessary to read it. To keep up with technological changes, regular migration of data is necessary for preservation purposes.

We have seen that libraries continue to be renovated, expanded, and replaced with new buildings that have attractive and comfortable interiors with provision for new technology. We have also seen that preservation activity exploded in the 1970s, first with a concern over brittle books, journals, and newspapers, and then more recently over the preservation of electronic information. One of the preservation concerns has been the need for better awareness and training in the profession. The next chapter traces the evolution of library education since 1945.

CHAPTER 8

Library and Information Science Education and Library Literature

Education for librarianship has gone through dramatic changes since World War II. In 1946, the standard professional degree was the BLS from a school of library science. Forty-five years later, it was a master's degree, often with "information" as well as "library science" in the title from a school that might not even have the word "library" or "library science" in its name.

The expansion and growth of libraries created an unprecedented demand for librarians in the 1950s and 1960s, leading to the establishment of 40 new accredited MLS programs up through the 1970s. But by the mid-1970s the demand for librarians disappeared and between 1978 and 1994, seventeen accredited MLS programs were closed. However, the remaining schools adapted to the times and even began expanding in the 1990s by cooperating or merging with related academic partners and/or expanding their programs in broader information studies—much to the discomfort of practitioners.

This chapter on LIS education is divided into the following units: the period of growth to the mid-1970s, the closing of MLS programs beginning in 1978, the integration of library science with information science, changes in the MLS curriculum, survival and growth of MLS programs in the 1990s and at the turn of the century, education of school library media specialists, tensions with practitioners, and doctoral study and research. This chapter also includes a brief historical survey of library literature.

A PERIOD OF GROWTH TO THE MID-1970s

One of the most significant developments in this period was the establishment of the MLS as the basic professional degree. The Denver Library School started this pattern by announcing such a program in May 1947 and graduating its first MLS students in June of 1948. Other library schools followed in quick succession. Before this time, the practice was a fifth-year BLS following four years of undergraduate college—or an undergraduate degree with a major in library science. At the 1948 ALA Midwinter Conference, a resolution was passed calling for professional library education only at the graduate level, with the master's degree being the first professional library degree to be earned.

The 1951 Accreditation Standards legitimized the MLS, and library schools began to offer "retread" programs to upgrade the former BLS degree holders into MLS degrees. In the meantime, Beta Phi Mu, the international library science honorary society, had been organized in 1948 and was beginning to grow rapidly.

In 1954, Dean Jesse Shera of the Western Reserve University library school established a Center for Documentation and Communication Research that began to conduct research in newly developing, unconventional methods of information storage and retrieval as well as to sponsor conferences. It was the first library school research center. Others were to follow at Illinois (1961) and at UCLA, Berkeley, Pittsburgh, and Indiana (all in 1968).

Beginning in 1961, a new program of study—a sixth-year degree or certificate—appeared on the scene at Columbia. By 1968–1969, 18 other library schools also offered this program of one year of study beyond the MLS degree. By 2004, there were 30 post–master's certificate programs. The *Journal of Education for Librarianship* (now *Journal for Library and Information Science Education*) was also established in 1961.

The 1960s also saw the establishment of two-year library technician programs in community and junior colleges to help meet the desperate shortage of library workers. These technical assistants were seen as relieving librarians of nonprofessional responsibilities, as well as helping to staff rapidly growing libraries. By 1967, a Council on Library Technical Assistants was established (later changed to Media

Technical Assistants) and, by 1970, 78 schools were offering library technician training.

Three important events occurred in 1965. Most important was the passage of the Higher Education Act, with Title II-B providing funds for library training in two parts: (1) training institutes and fellowships for MLS, sixth-year, and doctoral study; and (2) grants for research and demonstration. From 1966–1967 through 1970–1971, a total of 2,337 fellowships were awarded, of which 700 were at the doctoral level. During the same period, more than $12,000,000 was appropriated for library and information science research and demonstration.

There was an important Airlie House Conference in 1965 on Education for Information Science that was staged by the American Documentation Institute under the sponsorship of the U.S. Office of Education. Librarians attended this conference and were awakened to the implication of the computer for libraries. There was a focus away from microphotography on the part of documentalists toward "information science" at and after this conference.

The year 1965 also saw the establishment at ALA of an Office for Library Education through a grant from the H. W. Wilson Foundation. From this office, headed by Lester Asheim, came the policy statement "Library Education and Manpower," approved by ALA on June 30, 1970. The statement defined the first professional degree for all librarians as being the master's and indicated that henceforth the title "librarian" should no longer be used indiscriminately to designate all who work in libraries.

In 1972, there were new MLS accreditation standards in terms of the goals and objectives as defined by the MLS program itself. Standards on curriculum, faculty, students, governance, administration and finance, physical resources, and facilities were interpreted by clearly defined goals and specific objectives for the program for which accreditation was sought.

From 1946 to 1970, the entire period was characterized by a great shortage of librarians. A June 15, 1945, *Library Journal* article declared that 18,000 librarians were needed. In 1947, there were 2,232 openings at the ALA Conference Placement Center and only 401 registrants possibly looking for job (most already having one). In the same year, ALA estimated that 64,160 librarians would be needed between

1947 and 1960. In 1965, the ALA's *National Inventory of Library Needs* estimate was for 100,000 librarians. By 1966, the shortage was acute enough for the *New York Times* to begin running a special classified section for librarians.

In response, there was a dramatic increase in the number of library schools. In 1946, there were 36 accredited schools that awarded 1,072 degrees. By 1971, 7,696 MLS degrees were awarded by 51 accredited programs. Table 8.1 shows that 24 new accredited MLS programs were established by 1970.

Table 8.1.   New Accredited MLS Programs 1945 to Date (year discontinued)

1946	Catholic, Western Michigan (1983)
1951	Florida State, Indiana, Texas
1954	Rutgers
1960	UCLA
1961	Kent
1962	Pittsburg*
1965	Hawaii, Maryland, N. Texas, Wayne
1966	Oregon (1978)
1967	Missouri, N. Illinois (1994), San Jose
1968	Brigham Young (1993), Queens
1969	Iowa, Long Island, Rhode Island
1970	Southern Connecticut
1972	Alabama, Arizona, Buffalo, South Carolina, Tennessee
1973	Alabama A&M (1981), N.C. Central, S. Florida
1974	Clarion, St. Johns, Wisconsin—Milwaukee
1978	Ball State (1985), S. Mississippi
1979	Mississippi (1984)
1980	North Carolina at Greensboro
1988	Puerto Rico

*Transferred from Carnegie Institute of Technology

But with the beginning of the 1970s, the need for librarians lessened, as shown by the data in table 8.2.

Table 8.2.   Available Library Positions at the ALA Annual Conference—Placement Center (Rounded Off to Nearest Hundred)

	Applicants	Jobs
1968	600	1,600
1969	600	1,400
1970	900	900
1972	1,400	600
1974	1,900	400

The total number of advertisements for professional library positions in *American Libraries* and *Library Journal* are another indication of this trend (see table 8.3).

Table 8.3. Available Positions Advertised in *American Libraries* and *Library Journal*, 1961–1975

1961	2,826
1963	3,159
1965	3,673
1967	4,401
1969	3,171
1971	1,505
1975	1,071

But the growth of new MLS programs continued, as seen in table 8.1, with 15 new programs receiving initial accreditation between 1972 and 1980.

Table 8.4 shows the MLS programs that lost and then regained their MLS accreditation during the postwar period, and table 8.5 shows the programs initially accredited before World War II and continued with their MLS accreditation.

Table 8.4. MLS Programs Losing and Regaining Accreditation

School	Initial Program	Reaccreditation
Dominican	1936–1957	1960–
Emporia	1930–1958	1964–
NY Albany	1930–1959	1965–
NY Geneseo	1944–1959	1966–1983

Table 8.5. Programs Accredited before 1945

School Program	Years of Accreditation
Drexel	1924–
Illinois	1924–
Pratt	1924–
Simmons	1924–
Washington	1924–
Wisconsin	1924–
Michigan	1926–
Syracuse	1928–
Oklahoma	1930–
LSU	1932–
North Carolina	1932–
Texas Women's	1936–
Kentucky	1940–

THE CLOSING OF MLS PROGRAMS

The year 1978 marked the first closing of an MLS program, a trend that was to continue into the early 1990s. Table 8.6 shows the 17 MLS programs that were closed between 1978 and 1994. Seven of these were from among the 39 new MLS programs that had been established since World War II. Among them were the distinguished programs at Chicago and Columbia.

Table 8.6.   Closed Accredited MLS Programs (1978–1994) with Original Date of Accreditation

1978	Oregon (1966)
1981	Alabama A&M (1973)
1983	Geneseo (1944–1956, 1966–1983)
1983	Western Michigan (1946)
1984	Mississippi (1979)
1985	Ball State (1978)
1985	Denver (1932)*
1986	Minnesota (1933)
1986	Case Western Reserve (1924)
1988	S. California (1936)
1988	Emory (1924)
1988	Peabody Vanderbilt (1930)
1990	Chicago (1932)
1992	Columbia (1925)
1993	Brigham Young (1968)
1994	Berkeley (1924)
1994	N. Illinois (1967)

*Reaccredited in 2003

The primary cause of closed MLS programs was dropping enrollment due to low demand for librarians and fewer jobs. The peak year in terms of MLS graduates was 1973–1974, with 8,134 graduates. By 1985–1986, MLS graduates dropped to 3,564. During 2002–2003, there were 5,314 MLS graduates (see table 8.7).

Table 8.7.   Number of U.S. Accredited MLS Programs

1960	32
1970	49
1980	62
1990	52
2000	49
2005	49

But there were also other reasons for the closings. LIS schools were small in comparison to other schools and colleges on each campus. Those with no undergraduate presence (the majority) had little on-campus visibility. Their alumni were not wealthy. In times of budget crisis, they were sometimes judged as not being central to the home institution's mission. In short, they were isolated and vulnerable. At private universities, they could rarely support themselves and had to depend on subsidies.

As the writing of this work was being concluded, still another program was shut down after a ten-year hiatus. The School of Library and Information Studies at Clark Atlanta University closed in May of 2005—as a result of a new president who cut five academic programs to reduce a deficit of $7.5 million and ensure the survival of the university. However, the MIS program at the University of Denver, which was closed in 1985, was reaccredited in 2003.

INTEGRATION WITH INFORMATION SCIENCE

Since the mid-1960s, there was a gradual integration of a whole new discipline—information science—into the field of library science. Library and information science eventually became an interdisciplinary field. *Information science* was a term that first appeared in the late 1950s in a movement that broke away from the documentalist focus on microphotography toward computerized information storage and retrieval.

Librarianship was considered a profession concerned with the records of society, providing access to them and their content through a body of techniques and processes. Information science was a study of properties of recorded symbols, of the means by which they were processed, or the study of information processes in any information system in which they occurred.

Librarians and documentalists first signaled this integration at the Airlie House Conference of 1965. The American Documentation Institute became the American Society for Information Science in 1970. The growing union was seen in publications such as the *Annual Review of Information Science and Technology* (1966) and *Library Research* established in 1979, but changed to *Library and Information Science Research* in 1983. Another sign of this shift was the change in the name of the Association of American Library Schools (AALS). In 1983, this became the Association for Library and Information Science Education (ALISE).

The change was gradual in library education. When a new library school was established at the University of Pittsburgh in 1969, its title was the Graduate School of Library and Information Sciences. The new school at the University of Maryland in 1965 was called the School of Library and Information Services. In 1966, a new MLS program at the University of Missouri was called the School of Library and Information Science, and, by 1967, the newly established school at the University at Buffalo placed the emphasis on "information" with the title of "School of Information and Library Studies." In 1974, Syracuse was the first to drop "library" when it became the School of Information Studies. In 1980, 39 of the 62 accredited MLS programs were still called schools or departments of library science. By 1990, only five remained: the School of Library Service at Columbia, the School of Library Science at Southern Mississippi, the School of Library Science at Kent, the Library Science Program at Wayne, and the Graduate Library School at Arizona.

By 2000, there were none. Indeed, by the year 2004, 12 of the 45 U.S. accredited schools did not have either "library science" or "library" in their official title. Eighteen of the accredited programs were a department or school within a larger body such as a college, along with other related descriptions. The remaining were freestanding schools.

Those units without the word "library" in their titles were most often called college or school of information studies, but there were other titles as well: School of Information, School of Information Science and Policy, School of Information Sciences and Technology, the Information School, and School of Informatics.

CHANGES IN MLS CURRICULUM

The MLS curriculum has changed dramatically during the period under study. As an example, MLS courses at Western Reserve University during 1951–1952 included two semesters of Cataloging, two semesters of Reference Information Sources, and two semesters of a course called

Books and Readers. There were also courses dealing with library administration, the history of the book, and of the history of American libraries. A newly developed course called Documentation was offered as an elective. There was also a required research methods course and a thesis, probably to legitimize the new MLS taking the place of the former BLS degree. Most MLS programs phased out the thesis requirement by the late 1960s.

As with almost every aspect of librarianship, the advances in computer and communication technology also had a great impact on library and information science education. The advent of library automation, databases and online searching, the Internet and the Web, electronic publishing and digital libraries—all affected curricula and programs of study. So did the changing role of the library as a source for access to information outside the library building.

During the earlier decades in the post–World War II period, the preparation for librarianship was thought of as a five-year program. A four-year undergraduate degree in liberal arts and sciences was capped by a fifth year of professional preparation with the MLS degree. Later, other undergraduate degrees were acceptable, particularly for subject specialization. Then information science courses were added to curricula, and undergraduate programs in information science were also introduced.

In the early 1980s, the ALA commissioned a study of LIS competencies entitled *New Directions in Library and Information Science Education.* The competencies were grouped under functions and settings. Functions included acquisitions, cataloging and classification, circulation, collection development, indexing and abstracting, interlibrary loan, management, reference and serials control. Settings included academic libraries; public libraries; school libraries; legal, medical, corporate, and other special libraries; museums, archives, and publishing; database; and information centers.

A study by J. Beheshti in 1999 provided an overview of the knowledge- and skill-based competencies taught in ALA-accredited programs in the late 1990s. The following were identified: technology, management, organization of information, searching and database development, collection development, mathematical methods and research, sociocultural aspects, non-print media, rare materials and conservation, sources of information, reference materials, archives, children's literature and services, and professional issues.

Karen Markey analyzed the websites of LIS schools in 2002 to determine new trends in curriculum and other areas. She found a strong trend toward information technology and a focus on users of information. The curricula remained strong in traditional course work seeking a better understanding of users, their information-seeking behavior, and the sources and services that libraries provide to general users as well as to special population groups. At the same time, new themes were found in LIS curricula. These included community information systems, competitive intelligence, human–computer interaction, information architecture, knowledge management, medical informatics, and natural language processing.

SURVIVAL AND GROWTH IN THE 1990s
AND AT THE TURN OF THE CENTURY

The MLS programs that survived the closings not only survived, but even prospered by the 1990s. They responded to new opportunities in the information field and repositioned themselves within their universities to take advantage of increasing societal concerns with information and technology. They revised their curricula, hired faculty from a variety of disciplines, and went into new areas of education. These included undergraduate programs in information science, new master's programs in the research aspects of information science, joint degree programs, continuing education programs, and distance education programs using the new technologies. In the latter, they were often among the pioneers on their campuses.

The new 1992 accreditation standards were for master's programs in library *and* information science. For the first time, an institution could seek accreditation for more than one graduate program of education in library and information studies leading to a master's degree.

In 2000, the Kellogg-Alise Information Professions and Education Reform Project, funded by the W. K. Kellogg Foundation, examined recent changes in professional LIS programs. This important qualitative analysis by Pettigrew and Durrance described six major current trends in LIS education:

1. Schools were addressing broad-based information environments and problems.
2. Core curricula were predominately user centered and incorporated interdisciplinary perspectives.
3. Programs experienced an increased infusion of information technology.
4. Faculty were experimenting with structuring specializations.
5. Schools had diverse program formats.
6. Schools had expanded degree offerings at all levels.

In 2004, only three schools did not offer any distance education courses. Two schools offered entire master's programs through distance education.

EDUCATION OF SCHOOL LIBRARY MEDIA SPECIALISTS

Up through the period shortly after World War II, library education for school librarians was traditionally taught at teachers' colleges or colleges of education as part of an undergraduate degree in teacher preparation. Then it began to be offered as a special track within the MLS at library schools. In 2004, 44 out of the 48 accredited U.S. MLS programs offered a program leading to school library media certification.

Another avenue for school library media education was made available in 1988 when the ALA Council approved a policy recognizing a master's degree with a specialty in school library media from a National Council for Teacher Accreditation (NCATE) accredited program as an appropriate first professional degree for school library media specialists. In 1993, NCATE approved the first set of ALA/AASL "Curriculum Guidelines for the School Library Media Specialist Program." Revised standards were approved in 2003. By 2005, there were 34 NCATE-approved programs, with 27 of these at institutions that did not have ALA-accredited master's programs.

TENSIONS WITH PRACTITIONERS

There was always some degree of tension between practitioners and library educators. Practitioners were often critical because there was too much theory and not enough practical training in library and information science programs. Educators felt that there must be a balance between training and education. Then there was the question of what were the core and principal competencies that all MLS student should be taught. During the 1990s and until the present, the relationship has been turbulent, with the increasing emphasis on information science. There were accusations of abandonment of educating people to work in libraries. Some practitioners proposed that accreditation should not be granted to those schools that do not have the word "library" in their titles.

ALA stepped into the picture in 1999 with the first of three Congresses on Professional Education. The second congress was held in 2000 and the third in 2003. These were summits on library education that focused on initial preparation for librarianship, core competencies, post-MLS certification, continuing education, and support staff.

In the year 2001, ALA established an Allied Professional Association to provide leadership for the development, promotion, and improvement of the profession of librarianship and to certify individual librarians in areas of specialization beyond the ALA-recognized master's degree.

DOCTORAL STUDY AND RESEARCH

We have thus far emphasized the MLS but also need to examine doctoral programs in library and information science. Until 1948, the University of Chicago was the only school awarding the doctorate in library science. The first doctorate was bestowed by Chicago in 1930 and, by 1950, a total of 65 degrees had been awarded. After World War II, doctoral programs were established first at the University of Illinois and the University of Michigan in 1948 and then during the 1950s at Columbia, Case Western Reserve, and Berkeley. There are currently 29 U.S. schools offering a doctorate in library and information science. The PhD fellowships awarded under Title II-B of the Higher Education Act had an important impact on the growth of doctoral programs. During the first 20 years of this support, from 1966–1967 through 1985–1986, 1,058 fellowships were awarded for doctoral study.

Research methods in doctoral dissertations have changed greatly during the past 60 years. Historical/bibliographical and some descriptive methods were the research norm in the 1950s and 1960s. By the 1980s and 1990s, dissertations were divided by library and information science or just information science. There was a marked decline in the historical/bibliographical methods and a rise in a variety of research methods, including case study, bibliometrics, experimental, content analysis, modeling, and combinations of the above.

In 1945, there were few LIS faculty with doctorates and there was only one school—the University of Chicago—that was offering a PhD. Today, there are 29 schools with doctoral programs. Almost all of the current 783 full-time faculty have doctoral degrees.

LIBRARY LITERATURE

During the second half of the twentieth century, library literature grew tremendously. The *Library Literature* index volume for 1949–1951 lists 66 monographic publications in library science. By the year 2003, the *Bowker Annual* showed 529 books published in library and information science plus many more in related areas of information studies. The 1945 *Library Literature* volume indexed 46 U.S. library science journals plus some 14 international journals. The 2005 volume indexed 160 U.S. library and information science journals and 47 international journals.

Prior to World War II, there were three major library science publishers: the American Library Association, the H. W. Wilson Company, and R. R. Bowker LLC. Table 8.8 shows the major library science publishers established after World War II.

Table 8.8.   **Post–WWII Library and Information Science Publishers**

Scarecrow Press	1952
Shoestring Press	1952
Libraries Unlimited	1964
Greenwood Press	1967
Pierian Press	1967
Haworth Press	1975
Oryx Press	1975
Gaylord Professional Publications	1975
Neal-Schuman Publications	1976
Linworth Publishing	1982
Highsmith Press	1991

Among the most important new reference tools begun during this period were the *Bowker Annual of Library and Booktrade Information* (1956–), *Library Technology Reports* (1965–), the *Encyclopedia of Library and Information Science* (1968–2002 and 2003), and the *Dictionary of American Library Biography* plus supplements (1978–).

Table 8.9 lists the important new journals and serials that were also established.

Table 8.9.   Journals and Serials Established Post WWII.

American Documentation, now the *Journal of American Society of Information Science and Technology*	1950
Library Trends	1952
School Library Journal	1954
Library Resources and Technical Services	1957
RQ—now *Reference and User Services Quarterly*	1960
Journal of Education for Library and Information Science Education	1960
Information Processing and Management	1963
Choice	1964
Annual Review of Information Science and Technology	1966
Information Technology and Libraries	1966
Libraries and Culture	1966
Public Libraries	1970
Library and Information Science Research	1979
Journal of Academic Librarianship	1979
School Library Media Quarterly	1981

During the past 10 years, scholarly communication as well as the latest trends and developments in the field have also been increasingly covered through listservs, websites, and online journals. As an example, the *Katherine Sharpe Review* was founded in 1995 as a peer-reviewed e-journal devoted to student scholarship and research within library and information science. Another example is the *Informed Librarian Online,* begun in 2003, and providing a monthly compilation of the most recent tables of contents from LIS journals and newsletters, many of them full text.

We have seen that LIS education has had a turbulent history since 1945—first expanding greatly by raising the degree from a BLS to an MLS, then establishing many new schools to meet the seemingly insatiable demand for librarians up through the 1960s, and then contracting when that demand disappeared by closing many MLS programs. By the

1990s, LIS education met the challenge by adopting new technologies and new programs of study, and was beginning to prosper.

LIS research has also increased with the growth of doctoral programs and funding. This has been reflected by an increase in the number of journals, books, and electronic media being produced in library and information studies.

We now turn our attention to the products of this library education — the graduates. The next chapter covers the library leaders who made possible much of what we have covered up to this point. Not all were graduates of library education programs, but most were. Those who were not were closely related to the libraries and librarianship.

CHAPTER 9

Prominent Leaders in the Field of Libraries and Librarianship

Who were the most important and influential persons in librarianship during the period from the mid-1940s to the turn of the century? Who had the greatest impact on the development of the profession? Some names immediately come to mind. There is Jesse Shera, opinionated writer, scholar, and library educator. Certainly, Henriette Avram needs to be included for her development of the MARC format, and Fred Kilgour, founder and developer of OCLC. Bill Gates must be listed as a great library philanthropist. Others are not as easy to identify.

A systematic examination was made of prestigious awards to identify candidates for this selection. The following awards were presented during the past 60 years:

- ALA Honorary Membership (1879 to date) is bestowed on a person whose contribution to librarianship is so outstanding that it is of lasting importance to the advancement of the whole field of library service. It is intended to reflect honor on the ALA as well as on the individual.
- The Lippincott Award (1938 to date) is presented annually to a librarian for distinguished service to the library program.
- The Dewey Medal (1953 to date) is for recent creative leadership, particularly in fields in which Melvil Dewey was interested: library management, library training, cataloging and classification, and the tools and techniques of librarianship.
- The Beta Phi Mu Award (1956 to date) is given to a library school faculty member or to an individual for distinguished service to education for librarianship.

- The Isadore Gilbert Mudge-R. R. Bowker Award (1959 to date) goes to an individual for a distinguished contribution to reference librarianship.
- The Margaret Mann Citation (1951 to date) is for outstanding professional achievement in cataloging and classification.
- The American Association of School Librarians' AASL Distinguished Service Award (1978 to date) recognizes an individual member of the library profession who had, over a significant period of time, made an outstanding national contribution to school librarianship and school library development.
- The Association for Library Service to Children's ALSC Distinguished Service Award (1992 to date) is given to an ALSC member who had made significant contributions to and had an impact on library service to children and/or the ALSC.
- The Margaret E. Monroe Award (1986 to date) is to honor a librarian who has made a significant contribution to adult services.
- The ACRL Academic/Research Librarian of the Year Award (1979 to date) is for an outstanding member of the library profession who has made a significant national or international contribution to academic or research librarianship and library development.

With the exception of the Beta Phi Mu Award, all of the other honors mentioned above are given through ALA or its subdivisions.

In addition, the December 1999 issue of *American Libraries* was consulted to examine an article entitled "100 of the Most Important Leaders We Had." This covered the twentieth century, with the 100 leaders selected and described by the editorial staff of American Libraries based on their own study and research.

Finally, the *Dictionary of American Library Biography* (1978) was consulted. Here, an advisory board selects for inclusion those who had the greatest impact on U.S. librarianship and then selects the appropriate person to research and write the scholarly biographies. DALB goes back beyond the period of this study and is limited to those persons who are deceased. The 1990 and 2003 DALB supplements were also consulted.

An examination of all of the above awards and biographical sources resulted in some 60 possible candidates, but it was quickly discovered that not all areas of librarianship were being represented. The following additional awards or citation were also examined:

- The Marian Gould Gallagher Distinguished Service Award (1984 to date) in recognition of outstanding, extended, and sustained service to law librarianship
- The Music Library Association's Honorary Members (1965 to date)
- The Medical Library Association Fellows (1960 to date)
- The Special Libraries Association Honorary Members (1952 to date), the SLA Hall of Fame (1959 to date), and the SLA Professional Award (1949 to date)

Consultations with knowledgeable people in the above fields were also held by phone and e-mail.

The selection process was difficult. There were candidates who, while still living in the post–World War II period, made their major contributions before the World War II and were not included. Examples are Lucille Morsch, Joseph Wheeler, Keyes Metcalf, and Mildred Leona Batchelder.

Living candidates posed still another problem. Many current leaders in our field are still making contributions. Others could be recognized for great achievements already accomplished. My decision was to be sparing in selection for only truly outstanding contributions.

Emphasis was on librarians or those lay people closely associated with library development. Excluded were many contributors in documentation and later information science unless they had a direct impact on librarianship.

Finally, there were people who had a major impact but did not receive any or very few awards. They were still included in my listing.

Allain, Alex P. (1920–1994)

Library board member (1953–93) and chair (1975–1991) of the Franklin (Louisiana) Public Library. A vigorous intellectual freedom advocate who led the movement to establish ALA's Office of Intellectual

Freedom, cofounder of the Freedom to Read Foundation. A lawyer who acted as counselor on many key intellectual freedom cases.
ALA Honorary Member, 1975
American Libraries 100 Leaders, 1999
DALB Second Supplement, 2003

Arbuthnot, May Hill (1884–1969)

Prolific author about children's books. Her *Children and Books* (1947) was later published in six editions. ALA's Association for Service to Children sponsors an annual lecture in her name in recognition of her important contributions to children's literature and work with children.
DALB, 1978
American Libraries 100 Leaders, 1999

Asheim, Lester E. (1914–1997)

Made many contributions to library education, international librarianship, and intellectual freedom. Served as University of Chicago Library School faculty member, director of the ALA International Relations Office, director of the ALA Office for Education, and faculty member at the University of North Carolina, Chapel Hill library school.
Beta Phi Mu Award, 1973
ALA Lippincott Award, 1976
ALA Honorary Member, 1984
American Libraries 100 Leaders, 1999
DALB Second Supplement, 2003

Avram, Henriette (1919–2006)

Developed the MARC format while at the Library of Congress.
Margaret Mann Citation, 1971
Academic/Research Librarian Award, 1980
Dewey Medal, 1981
Lippincott Award, 1988
Special Libraries Association Professional Award, 1990

ALA Honorary Members, 1997
American Libraries 100 Leaders, 1999

Baker, Augusta (1911–1998)

Prominent children's librarian. After serving as a coordinator of children's services and storytelling specialist at the New York Public Library, she served as storyteller-in-residence at the University of South Carolina. Author and coauthor of anthologies of children's stories and books on storytelling.
ALA Honorary Member, 1975
American Libraries 100 Leaders, 1999
DALB, Second Supplement, 2003

Banks, Paul (1934–2000)

Pioneer in the field of library conservation and founder of a formal degree-training program in library and archival preservation/conservation at Columbia, later moving to University of Texas.
DALB Second Supplement, 2003

Berman, Sanford (1933–)

Passionate and outspoken advocate for reform in cataloging practice, using subject headings that would be more accessible to the patron. For many years, head cataloger at Hennepin County Library and one of the founders of *Alternative Library Literature.*
Margaret Mann Award, 1981
ALA Honorary Member, 2000

Bidlack, Russell E. (1920–2003)

Raised the stature of the library education program at the University of Michigan from a department to a school where he served as dean. A major force in the formulation of the 1972 standards of accreditation for the MLS.

Beta Phi Mu Award, 1977
Dewey Medal, 1979
ALA Lippincott Award, 1983

Carnovsky, Leon (1903–1975)

Served on faculty of the University of Chicago Library School with important contributions as scholar, author, and consultant. Produced many key library surveys.
Dewey Medal, 1962
Beta Phi Mu Award, 1971
ALA Lippincott Award, 1975
DALB, 1978
American Libraries 100 Leaders, 1999

Cheney, Francis Neel (1906–1996)

Noted library educator and reference specialist at the Peabody Library School (later Vanderbilt University).
Beta Phi Mu, 1959
Mudge Award, 1962
ALA Honorary Member, 1978
DALB Second Supplement, 2003

Clapp, Verner Warren (1901–1972)

After important service at the Library of Congress, he became the first president of the Council on Library Resources, where he stimulated library development in the 1960s by sponsoring major research and publications.
ALA Lippincott Award, 1960
ALA Honorary Member, 1967
DALB, 1978
American Libraries 100 Leaders, 1999

Clift, David H. (1907–1973)

Led ALA as executive director from 1951–1972 during a critical period of association and library growth.

ALA Lippincott Award, 1962
ALA Honorary Member, 1972
DALB, 1978
American Libraries 100 Leaders, 1999

Cooke, Eileen (1928–2000)

On staff of ALA Washington office from 1964–1993 and executive director from 1972–1993. Powerful lobbyist in convincing legislators about the importance of library funding and librarians about being politically active in fighting for this funding.
ALA Honorary Member, 1996
DALB Second Supplement, 2003.

Cunha, George Daniel Martin (1911–1994)

Director emeritus of the Northeast Document Conservation Center and former chief conservator at the Library of the Boston Athenaeum. A major authority on preservation of library and archival material. He spread the word about preservation through his teaching, mentoring, and counseling. His writings are classics in the field.

Dalton, Jack (1908–2000)

Important contributions as University of Virginia library director, head of the ALA International Relations Office, and dean of the University of Columbia Library School.
ALA Honorary Member, 1983
ALA Lippincott Award, 1984
DALB Second Supplement, 2003

Dixon, William S. (1910–1978)

Library director at Princeton University. Primary author of ALA's "Freedom to Read" statement. ALA president. Widespread recognition as a library leader and articulate spokesperson for the profession.
Dewey Medal, 1969

ALA Lippincott Award, 1971
ALA Honorary Member, 1978
DALB Supplement, 1990
American Libraries 100 Leaders, 1999

Dougherty, Richard M. (1935–)

Director of libraries at Berkley and at Michigan. Faculty member in library education at Michigan. ALA president. Founder and editor of the *Journal of Academic Librarianship*. Author and consultant in library management.
ACRL Academic/Research Librarian of the Year, 1983
ALA Lippincott Award, 1997

Downs, Robert B. (1903–1991)

One of the most prolific librarian-authors. Director of the University of Illinois libraries and library school for 27 years, where an annual intellectual freedom award is named for him. ALA president.
ALA Lippincott Award, 1964
Dewey Medal, 1974
ALA Honorary Member, 1976
American Libraries 100 Leaders, 1999
DALB Second Supplement, 2003

Edwards, Margaret (1902–1988)

Head of Young Adult Services at Enoch Pratt Free Library in Baltimore. A national force in services to young adults. There is a YALSA/ALA award in her name. Helped define services and outreach roles of young adult librarians in the United States.
American Libraries 100 Leaders, 1999
DALB Second Supplement, 2003

Ellsworth, Ralph Eugene (1907–2000)

Often referred to as the father of modern academic library buildings because of his publications and widespread service as a library building consultant. Also served as director of libraries at the University of Colorado and at the University of Iowa.

ALA Honorary Member, 1988

DALB Second Supplement, 2003

Fogarty, John E. (Hon.) (1913–1967)

Earned a place on the list by playing a major role in the passage of library federal legislation during the 1950s and 1960s as a member of Congress.

ALA Honorary Member, 1966

DALB, 1978

Gates, Bill (1955–)

Library philanthropist ranking next to Carnegie in prominence and generosity. Provided some $250,000,000 to public libraries for access to computers in low-income and disadvantaged communities and neighborhoods.

ALA Honorary Member, 1998 (along with Melinda Gates)

SLA Honorary Member, 2000

Gaver, Mary (1906–1992)

Advanced school library programs through her writings, teaching, and research. Helped develop school library standards. Taught at Rutgers University Library School. ALA president.

ALA Honorary Member, 1976

ALA-AASL Distinguished Service Award, 1980

American Libraries 100 Leaders, 1999

DALB Second Supplement, 2003

Gorman, Michael (1941–)

Dean of library services at California State University, Fresno. Editor of the second edition (1978) of *Anglo-American Cataloging Rules* and the 1988 revision. Author of hundreds of articles and books. ALA president.

Margaret Mann Citation, 1979
Dewey Medal, 1992

Henne, Frances W. (1906–1985)

Helped to establish ALA's American Association of School Librarians. First woman faculty member at the University of Chicago Library School, where she founded the Center for Children's Books. A leader in the development of school library standards.
ALA Lippincott Award, 1963
Beta Phi Mu Award, 1978
ALA/AASL Award, 1979
DALB Supplement, 1990
American Libraries 100 Leaders, 1999

Holley, Edward G. (1927–)

Leadership and contributions on a national level as scholar, university library administrator, library school dean, and educator. ALA president and consultant.
Dewey Medal, 1983
ALA Lippincott Award, 1987
ACRL Academic/Research Librarian of the Year, 1988
Beta Phi Mu Award, 1991
SLA Honorary Member, 1992

Jones, Virginia Lacy (1910–1984)

Served as dean of the Atlanta University Library School from 1945–1981. A respected leader and educator, mentor, and promoter of library access to black Americans.
Dewey Medal, 1973
ALA Lippincott Awards, 1977
Beta Phi Mu, 1980
ALA Honorary Member, 1983
DALB Supplement, 1990
American Libraries 100 Leaders, 1999

Josey, E. J. (1924–)

Led movement to desegregate ALA state chapters, founded ALA Black Caucus, author and library educator at University of Pittsburgh. Eminent and distinguished black librarian with five honorary doctoral degrees. ALA president.
ALA Lippincott Award, 1980
ALA Honorary Member, 2002

Kilgour, Frederick G. (1914–2006)

Founding director of OCLC, which revolutionized library growth and development as a nationwide computerized library network.
Margaret Mann Citation, 1974
Dewey Medal, 1978
ALA/ACRL Academic/Research Librarian, 1979
ALA Honorary Member, 1982
Medical Library Association Fellow, 1984
SLA Honorary Member, 1986

Krettek, Germaine (1907–1994)

ALA Washington office director (1957–1972). Played a key role in continuing and obtaining new federal funding during the 1960s.
ALA Lippincott Award, 1969
ALA Honorary Member, 1973
DALB Second Supplement, 2003

Krug, Judith F. (1940–)

Director of the ALA's Office of Intellectual Freedom since it was founded in 1967. Also helped to found the Freedom to Read Foundation and has served as its executive director since 1969. Has advised hundreds of libraries in dealing with challenges to library material. No person is more closely identified with libraries and the cause of intellectual freedom than Judith Krug.
ALA Lippincott Award, 1998

Lubetzky, Seymour (1898–2003)

LIS professor at UCLA. Foremost cataloging theorist of the 20th century.
Margaret Mann Citation, 1955
Dewey Medal, 1977
ALA Honorary Member, 2002

Lyman, Helen Huguenor (1910–2002)

Internationally recognized for her seminal study of adult education in U.S. public libraries in the mid-1950s and for her publications on the public library's role in adult literacy in the 1970s. Served as LIS faculty member at Wisconsin-Madison and then as adjunct professor at the University at Buffalo, where she taught until the age of 88.
ALA Lippincott Award, 1979
Margaret Monroe Award, 1986

Martin, Lowell (1912–)

Widely known and respected library educator, author, and consultant. Served on Columbia University LIS faculty and as the first LIS dean at Rutgers. Author of many important publications and reports dealing with public libraries.
ALA Honorary Member, 1979

McCook, Kathleen de la Pena (1948–)

Most recently dean of the University of South Florida LIS School and now distinguished university professor. Chief author of *Adult Services: An Enduring Focus for Public Libraries* (1980), a major study of adult services in the United States. Coauthor of another landmark book, *The Role of Women in Librarianship, 1876–1976* (1979). Many other important works. Also a proponent of diversity and equity in the profession.
Margaret E. Monroe Award, 1991
Beta Phi Mu Award, 2003

Metcalf, Keyes Dewitt (1889–1983)

Served as director of the New York Public Library and of the Harvard University Library. Upon his retirement in 1955, continued his professional accomplishments as a library educator at Rutgers and Columbia, as a library building design expert, and as a consultant right up to his death at the age of 94. Was awarded 12 honorary doctorates. ALA president.

ALA Honorary Member, 1963
ALA Lippincott Award, 1966
DALB Supplement, 1996
American Libraries 100 Leaders, 1999

Moon, Eric (1923–)

Major impact as *Library Journal* editor, as president of Scarecrow Press, and as president of ALA.

ALA Lippincott Award, 1981
ALA Honorary Member, 1987

Powell, Lawrence Clark (1906–2001)

Former director of the UCLA Library and founding dean of the UCLA library school. Then served on University of Arizona LIS faculty. Eminent educator, scholar, author, and bibliographer. Much in demand as a speaker and writer about the magic of books and libraries.

ALA Honorary Member, 1981

Ristow, Walter (1908–2006)

Most influential figure in U.S. map librarianship. A prolific cartographic scholar. Served as head of the New York Public Library Map Division and later chief of the Library of Congress Map Department.

Rollins, Charlemae (1897–1979)

Very influential African American children's librarian and author at the Chicago Public Library. Fought against inaccurate portrayal of blacks in children's books.

ALA Honorary Member, 1972
DALB Supplement, 1990
American Libraries 100 Leaders, 1999

Sayers, Frances Clarke (1897–1989)

Received national recognition for her leadership in strengthening library service to children. One of the most influential children's librarians of her generation. Noted author.
ALA Lippincott Award, 1965
American Libraries 100 Leaders, 1999
DALB Second Supplement, 2003

Shaw, Ralph R. (1907–1972)

Eminent scholar, bibliographer, inventor, teacher, and consultant. Founder of Scarecrow Press. Served at Rutgers as LIS faculty member and dean. Founding dean at the University of Hawaii. Innovative leader. ALA president.
Dewey Medal, 1953
ALA Honorary Member, 1971
DALB, 1978
American Libraries 100 Leaders, 1999

Shera, Jesse H. (1903–1982)

Eminent educator, philosopher, theoretician, and library historian. Dean of the Western Reserve LIS School, where he established the Center for Documentation and Communication Research in the emerging field of information retrieval.
Beta Phi Mu Award, 1965
Dewey Medal, 1968
ALA Lippincott Award, 1973
ALA Honorary Member, 1976
DALB Supplement, 1990
American Libraries 100 Leaders, 1999

Shores, Louis (1904–1981)

Educator who introduced audiovisual materials into library collections and founding dean of the Florida State University Library School.
Mudge Award, 1967
Beta Phi Mu Award, 1967
DALB Supplement, 1990

Stone, Elizabeth W. (1918–2002)

LIS dean at Catholic University. ALA president and major voice and leader in the spread of continuing education for librarians.
ALA Lippincott Award, 1986
ALA Honorary Member, 1988
SLA Professional Award, 1988
Beta Phi Mu Award, 1998

Tauber, Maurice (1908–1980)

Noted for coordinate indexing, library technical services, and as writer, researcher, educator, and administrator. Served on Columbia LIS faculty. Noteworthy publications on university library administration and on technical services. Produced many library surveys.
SLA Professional Award, 1952
Margaret Mann Award, 1953
Dewey Medal, 1955
DALB Supplement, 1990

Thomas, Lucille Cole (1921–)

Notable contributions as a school librarian, educator, and library trustee. Leadership role on local, state, national, and international levels. Began her career as a school librarian in New York City, where she rose to supervisor of school libraries and then director of the office of library, media, and telecommunications. Many leadership positions in ALA and president of the International Association of School Librarianship.

AASL Award, 1984
ALA Honorary Member, 2003

Vosper, Robert Gordon (1913–1994)

Worldwide recognition for the rights of librarians as partners in scholarly enterprise, and as UCLA library director. A leader in international librarianship. ALA president.
ALA Lippincott Award, 1985
ALA Honorary Member, 1993
American Libraries 100 Leaders, 1999
DALB Second Supplement, 2003

Wedgeworth, Robert (1937–)

Led ALA as executive director during crucial times from 1972–1985. Served as Columbia University LIS dean from 1985–1992 and as University of Illinois director of libraries from 1993–1999. IFLA president from 1991–1997. Five honorary doctorates.
ALA Lippincott Award, 1984
Dewey Medal, 1997

Wright, Louis B. (1899–1984)

Director of the Folger Shakespeare Library in Washington, D.C. Played key role in the establishment of the Council on Library and Information Resources because of his close contacts with the Ford Foundation.

The following persons played leading roles in the special library field and in the Special Libraries Association during the last half of the twentieth century:

David Bender
William Buddington
Elizabeth Ferguson
Robert W. Gibson, Jr.

Robert W. Gonzalez
Ruth Hooker
James Humphrey III
Eugene B. Jackson
Elizabeth U. Owen
Guy St. Clair
Winfred Swell
Rose Vormelker
Herbert White

Law librarianship has grown and developed since the late 1940s with the help of the following prominent librarians:

Robert Berring
Morris Cohen
Richard Danner
Elizabeth Finley
Marian Gallagher
Laura Gasaway
Frank Houder
Roger Jacobs
Julius Marke
Roy Mersky
Robert Oakley

In the medical library field, the following were the most distinguished librarians:

Harold Bloomquist
Alfred Brandon
Estelle Brodman
Lois Ann Colaianni
Louise Darling
Donald Lindberg
Nina W. Matheson
Irwin H. Pizer
Frank B. Rogers

The most influential librarian in music librarianship during the past
50–60 years were:

Ann Basart
Rita Benton
Carol June Bradley
Frank C. Campbell
Edward E. Colby
James B. Coover
Virginia Cunningham
Anna Harriet Heyer
Richard S. Hill
Irene Millen
Catherine Keyes Miller
Philip L. Miller
Ruth Watanabe

All of the persons named in this chapter made a substantial, positive
impact on the growth and development of libraries during 1945–2005.
All of the advances and accomplishments in the field of library and information science would not have been possible without their leadership and contributions. The next and final chapter summarizes and
highlights the major developments and advances of the field and looks
at current and future challenges.

CHAPTER 10

Summary and Conclusion

In this final chapter, the most important happenings and developments in libraries and librarianship since World War II are highlighted. This is followed by a description of current challenges facing our field. And finally, I conclude this work with an analysis of and personal views on the future status of libraries.

MAJOR EVENTS AND DEVELOPMENTS

In summary, then, what were the major trends and developments during the period from the end of World War II to the turn of the century? What were the most important events, the major forces, that shaped our profession until the beginning of the twenty-first century? Fifteen are listed. They are described below, not in order of importance, but rather in order of mutual relationships.

1. Tremendous Growth

First was the growth in numbers of libraries, librarians, associations, and library buildings—every numerical unit of library activity: from 25,000 libraries in 1948 to 126,000 libraries in the year 2005; from 58,000 librarians shown in the 1950 census to 190,000 librarians in the 2000 census. Eleven national library associations in 1948 grew to 56 associations by the turn of the century. Almost 9,000 public library buildings were built in the period from 1941–2004, with very few of these built during World War II. About 2,000 academic library buildings were erected between 1948 and 2004. The 1945 edition of the *American Library Directory* had 624 pages. The 2005–2006 edition, in two massive volumes, has 4,166 pages.

2. Information Explosion

The explosion of knowledge and the expansion of library collections from print, primarily books, to a wide range of information formats. Print resources grew dramatically. There were 11,000 book titles in print in 1970. By 2004, this number has risen to 171,061! In 1947, there were 7,500 journal titles. By 2005, this had risen to 186,100 titles.

Traditional collections grew tremendously, as shown in table 10.1 for some representative libraries.

Table 10.1.   Selected Libraries and Number of Volumes

Library	1950	2005
Library of Congress	8,960,000 volumes	29,000,000 volumes
Harvard University	5,400,000 volumes	15,181,000 volumes
University at Buffalo	250,000 volumes	3,331,000 volumes
SUNY College at Cortland	38,000 volumes	417,000 volumes

This explosion of print sources was joined by a dramatic expansion of other formats, ranging from microform to film, video, and DVD, from audio disks, cassettes, CDs, and DVDs, and from databases to digitized library collections.

3. Impact of Technology

The impact of technology did not start with computers during the period but with photochargers and thermofax copiers in the 1950s and later with IBM Selectric typewriters and Xerox copiers. Then came computers, library automation, the MARC record, commercial databases, online records, networking, the Internet, and the World Wide Web. All of the above revolutionized library operations and services, bringing about resource sharing and a shift from ownership to access. The Internet and World Wide Web, in particular, changed the way we publish, communicate, and access information. Remote access from the Web has revolutionized library service.

4. Federal Funding

The importance of federal aid to libraries—from $7,500,000 authorized by the Library Services Act of 1956 to $205,951,000 in 2005— accounted for many expanded programs. It all began with the establishment of the ALA Washington office in 1945 and the beginning of effective lobbying activities by capable ALA leadership both in Washington and at ALA headquarters in Chicago.

The effects of federal funding were often magnified by matching funds from state and local governments. Public libraries were the first to benefit but were later joined by grants to academic, school, and some special libraries. The benefits included thousands of new or expanded library buildings, the growth of library systems and consortia, scholarship aid to MLS and LIS PhD students, support for continuing education, and funds for research in LIS.

5. The Council on Library and Information Resources

The founding of the Council on Library Resources in 1956 was one of the key developments in our field. CLR (now CLIR) began with support for *Choice* magazine, ALA's Library Technology Project, the development of MARC, and the establishment of OCLC, and continues to be a major force in preservation activities and in the professional development and advancement of library leaders. An examination of grants in CLIR's annual reports reveals its involvement and positive influence on almost every aspect of our profession during the past forty years.

6. Library Cooperation

The establishment and growth of library systems, consortia, and networks from a handful of bibliographic centers in 1945 to 401 consortia and networks and 703 library systems by 2005 was a major development.

All of this began with the information explosion and the growing realization of the need to share resources. Public libraries began to form public library systems in the 1950s; a further stimulus occurred in the 1960s and 1970s with Title III of the Library Services and Construction Act, the development of the MARC record, and the establishment of OCLC and other bibliographic utilities.

In the late 1940s, most libraries stood alone. By the 1960s and 1970s, most began sharing resources as a member of one or more library systems or consortia. By the late 1990s, most had access to information resources that were worldwide.

7. Professional Associations

The growth and importance of library professional associations was a major trend. The increase in the number of associations was a reflection of the increasing specialization of the profession. Professional associations had a major impact throughout this period on almost every phase of library development. Their activities included lobbying for funding, promotion of libraries, development of library standards, accreditation of library education programs, publication of books and journals, offering continuing education, promoting diversity, defending intellectual freedom, developing technology, and sometimes taking stands on political and social issues affecting libraries and librarianship.

Indeed, in the view of some, we have tended to become too much involved in the workings of our professional associations (especially ALA) to the detriment of our time and energies, which might be better spent in promoting libraries and serving on community committees rather than on the 3,000 ALA committees, and talking and writing more to our users and community and policy leaders rather than to ourselves.

8. Intellectual Freedom

One of the major accomplishments of our field during the past 60 years, primarily through the ALA, has been a structure for the defense of intellectual freedom and the ability to organize against attempts at censorship of library information sources. This has become the bedrock of our profession. It began with the Library Bill of Rights in 1939, later amended in the postwar period. It continued during the McCarthy era in the 1950s, when libraries were under attack, and continues to this day with concern about the Patriot Act and the Children's Internet Protection Act. During the 1960s and 1970s, a number of institutions were formed that greatly helped the status of libraries: the Office for Intellectual Freedom, the Freedom to Read

Foundation, the LeRoy C. Merritt Fund, and the Intellectual Freedom Round Table, as well as the guidance and leadership of Judith Krug of the ALA Office for Intellectual Freedom.

9. Library Standards

A plethora of standards were produced by the profession from the late 1950s through the 1970s, followed by planning guidelines and procedures. Every type of library was affected. Standards for public libraries were issued in 1956 and 1966—for public library service to young adults in 1959, to children in 1961, and for audiovisual services in 1970. By the late 1970s and into the 1980s and 1990s, there was a shift from standards for public libraries to goals and objectives, measurement, evaluation, and planning.

Among academic libraries, there were college library standards in 1959 and 1975, junior college library standards in 1960 and 1972, university library standards in 1979, and again college library standards in 2000 and 2004.

School libraries issued a series of standards in 1960, 1969, and 1975, and then (like public libraries) shifted to guidelines and planning statements in 1988 and 1998.

Special libraries promulgated standards in 1964, and there were also standards for library service to the blind and visually impaired issued in 1966 and updated in 1980 and in 2005.

10. Diversity and Ethnicity

Greater diversity and the rising status of women and minorities were major developments with wide impacts.

This time period began when many libraries were still segregated, as were many Southern state library associations. By the mid to late 1960s, this was put to an end.

The period also began with over 80% of the profession being women, and so it has remained. But there has been progress in greater equality for women in compensation and advancement—particularly in upper levels of administration, which formerly had been monopolized by men.

There are also more black librarians in the profession as well as Hispanic, Asian American, and Native American—at all levels. The provision of federal fellowships at the MLS and PhD levels for minority students helped greatly to recruit good candidates—as did the ALA Spectrum Initiative scholarships. But more still remains to be done.

11. Preservation

Preservation began to have its greatest impact in the late 1960s. As library collections grew, particularly in the larger libraries, there was a growing concern over brittle books and newspapers. Microfilm was turned to as the salvation, and acid-free paper was adopted by most publishers. Deacidification techniques were developed. CLIR took the lead in the library preservation movement, as did the many libraries that appointed preservation officers and departments. Digital preservation came into the picture during the late 1990s.

12. LIS Education

There were great changes in the education of librarians, from the establishment of the MLS to the amalgamation with information science.

Library education has been an important force during the period. The MLS was firmly established by 1951 as the basic professional degree. Then, through the early 1970s, there was a severe shortage of librarians, which resulted in the establishment of many new schools. From the mid-1970s through the mid-1980s, the need for librarians diminished; for this and other reasons, 17 MLS programs were closed. During the 1990s, LIS programs responded to advances in information technology by expanding their programs beyond the MLS, and most have grown and become successful on their campuses.

This has caused increasing tension with the practitioners. There has always been some tension regarding how much theory versus practice should be covered. Now the tension is over MLS programs not providing the basics of librarianship in favor of broader information studies, and also over the disappearance of "library science" from the names for schools and degrees.

The recruitment and education of future librarians and library educators is a major challenge for MLS and doctoral programs. Two factors make this particularly important: a high level of retirement and the challenges of rapid change.

13. Professional Recognition

There was a growing national recognition and respect for libraries and librarianship during this period. It began with federal funding in 1956. National Library Week began in 1956 and continues to provide further visibility, as has the adoption of uniform signage for libraries on all roads and highways. This was followed in 1958 by the Association of University Professors (AAUP) welcoming academic librarians as faculty into its membership. The establishment of the National Commission on Libraries in 1970 and the White House Conferences on Libraries in 1979 and 1991 were further evidence of this recognition.

The information explosion and the growth of the information industry, plus the growing emphasis on the importance of information in our society, have also had some positive effects for libraries.

The explosive growth in the capacity, number, and power of computers, in telecommunication, and in the new media have made all of society information-conscious. On the one hand, there is a heightened recognition of the importance of libraries and librarians. But on the other hand, other professions see opportunities in the information world. New jobs are emerging in this information environment. And there are now many other information providers competing with libraries.

14. Shifts to Digital Formats and to Access

As the twentieth century was drawing to a close, two related events occurred: a shift from paper to digital form as the most important information medium, and a shift from building library collections to providing access to information for users from wherever that information was located. In the 5,000-year history of libraries, these two milestone events are equal in importance to the invention of printing in the fifteenth century. The library is still a storehouse but now is also serving as an intermediary and a gateway to a world of information.

At the same time, books are being produced in increasing numbers, and new library buildings are being built. Library usage and circulation figures continue to rise.

15. Leadership

All of these major events and developments could not have occurred without effective leadership. We have seen examples of this leadership and innovation in the biographical listings of chapter 9. There were many others who were not listed who made important contributions toward the progress made during the past 60 years.

CURRENT CHALLENGES

There are a number of challenges facing librarianship that we must address. One has to do with technology. Unfortunately, too many librarians are being intoxicated with the power and abundance of technology. By the turn of the century, there were numerous proposals being made for new titles for librarians, such as access engineer, cybrarian, information counselor, and information architect, along with already existing information specialist and information manager.

The emphasis on providing access and the infatuation with technology has at times made librarians ignorant and/or indifferent to user needs. What library users really want and need is individual guidance to quality information meeting their specific needs. Service has always been a basic belief and practice of our profession. We need to be constantly reminded of this belief. Information technology does not replace face-to-face instruction or counseling; it just facilitates these human interactions.

The Internet is not a substitute for the library or for the personal assistance described above. The Internet is marvelous, but it is not going to make libraries obsolete. Not everything is on the Internet, and there is no quality control. It is like a vast uncataloged library.

Another challenge is the need to concentrate on spreading not only computer literacy but also basic literacy—the ability to read and write in order to be able to function in modern society. We also need to promote reading, to help people become more knowledgeable through reading.

The above can be accomplished through greater cooperation with literacy organizations and through library-sponsored activities such as exhibits, lectures by authors, book discussion groups, and the provision of reading promotion and guidance at the library and on library websites. In the eyes of the public, libraries are still associated with books and reading. We should not let technology overcome this relationship but rather capitalize on it. Libraries need to become centers of culture for gatherings and discussions.

The Library of Congress has done admirable work with the establishment of the Center for the Book in 1977. This has now spread to affiliate centers established in 50 states. The Center for the Book stimulates public interest in books, reading, and libraries, and encourages the study of the role of books and reading in society. Reading promotion, which includes combating illiteracy (the inability to read) and aliteracy (the lack of motivation to read), is the heart of the program.

Another challenge is the need to expand our work with children—the hallmark of our profession. Those librarians who work with the young in public and school libraries are the core of librarianship and, in my view, do more important work than most of us in the profession. They not only help to educate and inform at a critical age, but they also set the pattern for the way children will think about libraries for their entire lives.

We need to make sure that access to trained school media specialists with well-stocked libraries and to trained children's librarians in public libraries offering a host of story hours, reading programs, and similar events are considered essential. This important work is being carried out by 100,000 of the 120,000 libraries in operation—truly the core of our profession. A final challenge is the continuing need to provide free access to a full range of information representing all viewpoints to all segments of society, to all age levels, all income levels, and all education levels. This is another basic belief of libraries that we must continue to practice. It is not the view of many other information providers.

FUTURE STATUS OF LIBRARIES

First, it should be noted that there have been continuing predictions throughout this period of the end of books and/or libraries. It seemed that with each new technological development in information—such as the mass paperback book, television in the 1940s and 1950s, and the advent of computer use in the 1950s—there were such dire forecasts. As an example, the future of the book was hotly debated at the twentieth annual conference of the University of Chicago Library School in 1955. The same topic was chosen as the subject of the eighteenth R. R. Bowker Lecture at the New York Public Library in 1956. At about the same time, microforms were going to reduce the size of collections to a shoe box. As the 1960s ended, there were gloomy predictions of the end of public libraries.

It was also in the 1960s that there were predictions about a paperless society by the end of the century. In 1962, Marshall McLuhan published *The Gutenberg Galaxy* in which he claimed that nonprint media would lead to the elimination of the print era. In 1980, F. Wilfred Lancaster in his *The Impact of the Paperless Society on Research Libraries of the Future* predicted the decline of the book, with replacement by electronically accessible forms of information and a paperless society. In James Thompson's *The End of Libraries* (1982) the message was that computers would displace our "book-centered communal memory." And, in 2003, Charles Martell, in an article entitled "Role of Librarians in the Twenty-First Century," which appeared in the new *Encyclopedia of Library and Information Science,* declared that cyberspace would emerge victorious and that the library would diminish in importance.

When trying to predict the future of libraries, one must take into account the great variety of libraries. All may have the same general goal of selecting appropriate information source and organizing and making them available with assistance to their users, but they perform this function differently. One cannot evaluate, characterize, or predict for all of them. There is a tendency for scholars both in and outside the field to predict in terms of academic and, especially, research libraries because those same scholars are in that environment and may not be familiar with other kinds of libraries. As important as research libraries may be, they represent only about 2% of the 126,000 libraries in the United States. There are wide differences among the following libraries, as examples:

A small rural public library without a professional librarian
Medium-sized suburban public libraries

An inner-city branch library
Central library of a large city
Community college library
Four-year college library
A major research university library
A library media center in a centralized rural school with grades K–12
A library media center in a school located in a wealthy suburb
A library media center in an inner-city school
A library media center in a private school

And there would be differences between a special library serving a for-profit organization and one serving a nonprofit.

And then there is Harvard University, with its ninety libraries containing over 15,000,000 volumes and adding over 200,000 volumes per year. Contrast this with the majority of small public libraries with an average of 50,000 volumes in their collection and perhaps adding 2,000 volumes per year.

Harvard's collections are there to meet the curricular and research needs of its students and faculty and also to help preserve the historical record of our civilization. Most public libraries meet the current information, educational, and recreational needs of their residents with perhaps some concern for preserving local history.

And so predictions for the future by those who are primarily speaking for research libraries may have little consequence for the vast majority of U.S. libraries. The major core of the field is in the vast number of school and public libraries—over 100,000 libraries serving over 80 percent of all library users.

In thinking about the future, one must bear in mind that the history of libraries during the past 5,000 years has been a history of constant change, and always in relationship to political, economic, social, and cultural events occurring at the same time. Libraries do not operate in a vacuum but are affected by events around them.

If one traces the almost 5,000 years of library history beginning with clay tablet collections in Mesopotamia around 2,700 B.C.E. down through Egypt, Greece, Rome, and the medieval age to the present, there is evidence of constant change in the contents of libraries, their location, and in the role of librarians.

The content of collections has evolved from clay tablets to wood, papyrus scrolls, silk, parchment, and paper and print (fifteenth century). The evolution continued to microfilm, audio recordings, film, CD-ROM, video, DVD, computer databases, Internet, and the Web.

The location of libraries has varied from temples to monasteries, churches, bookmobiles, Erie Canal book boats, cruise ships, and to deposit collections in rural villages. For the first 3,000 years, with very few exceptions, collections were very small and generally accessible to only limited users and not in buildings of their own.

The status of librarians has also evolved from high priest to civic official, to slave librarian in the time of Rome, to scholar librarian, and to professional librarians trained in a special program—just 120 years ago with the founding of School Library Economy by Melvil Dewey at Columbia University in 1887.

A look back over 5,000 years of library history will also show that libraries have survived floods, fires, tyrants, pillaging, vandals, inquisitions, revolutions, wars, book burnings, censorship attacks, budget crises, and, as we have seen, predictions of their demise. Libraries have constantly adapted to challenge and change during these 5,000 years—sometimes slowly—but they have survived and grown.

Libraries and librarians will survive the latest challenges. They have already done so with the incorporation of computer technology—through MARC, with road maps to the Internet linking researchers to sites of respectable quality, and with library education responding to a poor job market and closings by incorporating information science into their curricula and expanding programs and degree offerings.

We need to continue to respond with boldness, adaptability, and creativity. We cannot ignore our new competitors in this information society but must work with them as partners—make use of their expertise, share our expertise with them, and hold fast to our important role—indeed, we must play a leadership role in the information world. Communication systems are continually changing the way people access information. Technology is also continually replacing itself. We need to keep up with these changes.

And so libraries will survive and grow, although they will be different. In the immediate future, digital media will not overwhelm all other media in libraries. Libraries will continue to collect and acquire, preserve, organize, and make available through expert assistance the entire universe of formats ranging from print to nonprint, with increasing accessibility by means of computers to collections or information resources worldwide. The physical library will endure but the services will continue to expand beyond the walls—and librarians may also operate outside the library building as expert guides to the vast, complex world of information.

We have come a long way in 5,000 years. An attempt has been made to cover only 60 of these years, but they have been important decades of dramatic change and progress. Future historians will undoubtedly look back upon this period as one having a greater impact than the one that witnessed the invention of printing.

Chronology

Three chronologies are provided: one listing the major historical events from 1944 to 2005, the second showing the technological advances during this period, and the third enumerating major occurrences and developments specifically in libraries and librarianship. The first two chronologies provide a background for what was happening in society as we traced library development from the end of World War II to the present.

CHRONOLOGY—GENERAL HISTORY

1944   Serviceman's Readjustment Act (GI Bill) is passed allowing millions of returning veterans to seek higher education.

1945   End of World War II

1946   Benjamin Spock's *Baby and Child Care* is published. Many editions followed. Used extensively as a guide for child care in postwar period.

1947   Levittown, Long Island, a planned suburban community, is established. Led trend to suburban growth.

1948   Four million autos produced.

1949   First credit card (Diner's Club).

1950   U.S. population is 150,697,361. Korean War begins. Establishment of National Science Foundation.

1953   Department of Health, Education, and Welfare is established

1954   *Brown vs. Board of Education*—School segregation is declared illegal.

1955   Rosa Parks begins Montgomery, Alabama, bus boycott. Ray Kroc franchises McDonald's. Disneyland opens.

1960   U.S. population grows to 178,464,236. FDA approves birth control pill.

1963   Assassination of President John F. Kennedy. *The Feminine Mystique* by Betty Freidman is published.

1964   Civil Rights Act is approved.

1965   Voting Rights Act is passed. Medicare is established.

1966   National Organization for Women is founded.

1967   First microwave oven is introduced.

1968   Martin Luther King is killed.

1969   Stonewall riot begins struggle for gay rights. Humans walk on the moon.

1970   U.S. population reaches 203,302,031.

1973   *Roe vs. Wade* decision allows abortion.

1976   U.S. bicentennial is celebrated.

1979   U.S. Department of Education is established.

1980   Population is now 226,542,199.

1985   Mikhail Gorbachev becomes USSR leader, tries to reform communist rule.

1989   Led by Poland, communist regimes collapse in Central and Eastern Europe.

1990   U.S. population is 248,709,873. First Gulf War begins.

1991   Breakup of the Soviet Union.

2000   Population reaches 281,421,906.

2001   9/11; the war against the Taliban in Afghanistan.

2003   U.S. topples Saddam Hussein in Iraq.

2006   U.S. population is 300,000,000.

CHRONOLOGY—TECHNOLOGY

1946   ENIAC, the first fully developed computer, is introduced.

1947   The transistor is invented.

1948   Long-playing records appear.

1949   First 45 RPM phonodisc is available.

1951   UNIVAC computer is introduced. Color TV appears.

1957   The USSR launches Sputnik. First stereophonic phonodiscs.

1958   The first U.S. satellite is launched. NASA is established.

1959   Xerox automatic copier is made available. First microchip in use.

1960   Printed circuits developed.

1964   BASIC computer programming language is written.

1969   ARPANET network, forerunner of the Internet, is set up by Defense Department.

1970   Floppy disk is invented.

1972   Intel produces first microprocessor. ORBIT, DIALOG, and INFOBANK are launched.

1974   First successful retail bar-code reader is introduced.

1975   First videocassette recorder (VCR) is introduced.

1976   Apple Computer becomes available. Kurzweil reading machine becomes available.

1977   Bibliographic Retrieval Service (BRS) starts up.

1981   Personal computer (PC) is launched by IBM.

1982   Compact disc—first CD players are introduced.

1983   First data-bearing disk is produced.

1984   Macintosh introduced computers using "the mouse" concept.

1988   Pentium chip introduced by Intel. First inkjet printer is introduced.

1990   Microsoft Windows software is introduced.

1993   The World Wide Web becomes a practical possibility with the appearance of the Mosaic browser, followed by Netscape Navigator and Microsoft Explorer, making the WWW explode in popularity by 1995.

1994   PalmPilot is available.

1997   First DVD players available.

1999   P2P (peer-to-peer) networks.

2002   iPod is introduced.

2004   Podcasting.

CHRONOLOGY—LIBRARIES AND LIBRARIANSHIP

1945   *School Libraries for Today and Tomorrow.* The first library standards for K–12 paved the way for school library media centers of today.

National Plan for Public Library Service is published. ALA's Washington office is established.

1947 The Public Library Inquiry (Social Research Council with funding from the Carnegie Corporation) was carried out until 1952.

1948 Initiation of the Farmington Plan—collection responsibility for new foreign research materials was distributed among 60 research libraries.

Establishment of the Beta Phi Mu International Library Science Honor Society.

1949 The Midwest Interlibrary Center—later known as the Center for Research Libraries—was founded by 10 Midwestern universities with the following purposes: deposit of infrequently used material; cooperative purchase and centralized housing of rarely used material; coordination of acquisition to avoid unnecessary duplication.

ALA Cataloging Rules for Author and Title Entries and a companion volume, *Rules for Descriptive Cataloging in the Library of Congress,* are published.

1951 The American Library Association adopts new standards of accreditation, making the MLS the entry degree for professional positions.

King County public library in Seattle has first machine-produced book catalog, generated from punched cards.

1952 *Library Trends* begins publication.

1954 Dean Jesse Shera establishes the Center for Documentation and Communication Research at Western Reserve University School of Library Science—the first of its kind.

1955 The Presidential Libraries Act of 1955 is signed.

1956 The Council of Library Resources is established as a result of a 1954 Ford Foundation study into the needs of libraries and the relation of those needs to society. The findings recommended that a planning body, independent of other organizations, be created for a solution to various library problems. CLR became an incubator of ideas and coordinator of library development.

The American Association of University Professors advanced the move toward faculty status for librarians when they voted to admit librarians as members.

President Eisenhower signs the Library Services Act. First federal funding in support of librarians, specifically for extension of public library service to rural areas.

Public Library Service: A Guide to Evaluation is published. These standards promote sharing, cooperation, and public library systems.

1957 National Library Week is inaugurated with the slogan "Wake Up and Read." It continues to this day.

1959 First set of *Standards for College Libraries* is produced. In 1975, these standards were broadened to include staff and space as well as collections. *Standards for Work with Young Adults* is published.

1960 *Standards for School Library Programs* is published, showing the importance of nonprint materials.

Standards for Junior College Libraries is published. Superceded in 1972 by *Guidelines for Two-Year College Learning Resources Programs.*

RQ and *Journal of Education for Librarianship* begin to be published.

1961 ALA participates in the Seattle's World's Fair with a futuristic Library-21 exhibit with the support of the Council on Library Resources, the U.S. Office of Education, and business and industry.

The Council on Library Resources funds an 18-month school library development project aimed at developing school library leadership to implement national standards.

1962 Marshall McLuhan's *The Gutenberg Galaxy* predicts that nonprint media will lead to the elimination of the print era.

1963 *Choice* magazine was launched with the assistance of a $150,000 grant from the Council on Library Resources. Its mission was to select and review titles of greatest interest and need to college libraries, faculty, and students. Faculty served as reviewers in their subject specialties.

The Academic Facilities Act funded construction of academic library buildings at both public and private institutions of higher education.

Knapp School Libraries Project begins (1965–1974), selling the need for quality media programs by setting up model media programs throughout the country, developing library job descriptions (school library manpower project), and establishing six model school library media education programs at colleges and universities.

1964   ALA sponsors Library USA Exhibit during 1964 and 1965 at the World's Fair in New York City. First public demonstration of online bibliographic retrieval.

Passage of the Library Services and Construction Act, extending federal aid beyond rural areas. Reauthorized into the 1990s.

Title III of the above act called for the establishment and maintenance of local, regional, state, and interstate cooperative networks and for the coordination of information services of school, public, academic and special libraries, permitting the user of any one type of library to draw upon the others.

Objectives and Standards for Special Libraries is published.

Standards for Children's Services in Public Libraries becomes available.

The first electronic book theft detection system is installed in the Grand Rapids (Michigan) Public Library.

The *Standards for Library Functions at the State Level* is established.

1965   The Higher Education Act of 1965 provided assistance to libraries; Title II-A granted funds for acquisitions and networking at college libraries, and Title II-B provided funds for training of new and degreed librarians (through institutes) and research and demonstration projects, including the development of new ways of processing, storing, and distributing information.

For the first time, school libraries are part of federal legislation in the Elementary and Secondary Education Act.

National Endowment for the Arts and the National Endowment for Humanities are established.

J. C. R. Licklider's *Libraries of the Future* is published.

1966   The initiation of the MARC (machine-readable cataloging) project at the Library of Congress provided cataloging information in a machine-readable form. MARC II magnetic tapes are released in 1968.

Guidelines for Young Adult Services in Public Libraries is published.

President Johnson appoints a President's Committee on Libraries and a National Advisory Commission on Libraries.

The *Standards for Services to the Blind and Visually Handicapped* is adopted, updated in 1980.

1967   The Office on Intellectual Freedom is established by ALA.

OCLC is founded by Frederick Ralph Kilgour as a consortium of 49 academic libraries in Ohio. The primary objectives were resource sharing and reduction in per-unit library costs.

Stanford University begins development of BALLOTS—Bibliographic Automation of Large Library Operations Using a Time-sharing Unit System.

Books for College Libraries is published as a guide for what should be in library collections.

Introduction of the Standard Book Number (SBN)—later ISBN.

Anglo-American Cataloguing Rules is completed in two versions, a North American text and a British text, which helps advance cooperation by encouraging the spread of shared cataloging.

The American Documentation Institute (founded in 1937) changes its name to the American Society for Information Science.

Minimum Standards for Public Library Systems is published.

1968   The Library of Congress begins publishing the *National Union Catalog of Pre-1965 Imprints,* which totals 754 volumes when completed in 1981.

1969   ARPANET links U.S. researchers and academic institutions. The Advance Research Project Agency (ARPA) was a resource-sharing computer network that became known as ARPANET, a wide-area packet-switching network, which later evolved into the Internet.

Standards for School Media Programs is issued. The unity of print and nonprint materials is emphasized.

First edition of *Introduction to Reference Work* by William A. Katz is published.

The Freedom to Read Foundation is established.

1970   ALA Task Force on Women is created.

Social Responsibilities Round Table is established within ALA.

Establishment of the National Commission on Libraries to provide every individual in the United States with equal opportunity of access to needed information regardless of location, social or physical condition, or level of intellectual achievement.

Guidelines for Library Service in Healthcare Institutions is published by ALA.

Black Caucus of the American Library Association is established.

Ohio State University launches online public access catalog.

1971   The Cataloging in Publication Project (CIP) is introduced by the Library of Congress.

The OCLC shared cataloging system is made available online in the state of Ohio. In 1978, it is made a national system. First online bibliographic utility.

The National Library of Medicine establishes the MEDLINE national database for health science researchers.

1972   ALA's Committee on Accreditation establishes revised standards of accreditation for MLS programs requiring each to have clear and stated goals and objectives.

Preservation as a formal library function is introduced at Yale University, at the New York Public Library, and at Columbia University.

Stanford University's BALLOTS is earliest successful integrated library system.

1973   The Lexis legal research system is made available commercially.

National Legislative Day is established by ALA and continues to this day.

1974   The Research Libraries Group (RLG) is founded as an alternative to institutional self-sufficiency during a period of tremendous publishing output and rising costs.

1975   (mid-1970s) CLSI, the first turnkey library system vendor, began to sell libraries an entire circulation system based on a Digital Electronics Corporation microcomputer.

1976   Copyright Act of 1976 (first revision since 1909), with significant provisions for libraries.

ALA and *Library Journal* are 100 years old.

1977   The Center for the Book is established at the Library of Congress to stimulate public interest in books, reading, literacy, and libraries, and to encourage the study of books and the printed word.

ALA reaffirms its support for free access in opposition to "fee for service."

Direction for Library Services to Young Adults is published, revised in 1993 and 2002.

Controversy over *The Speaker,* a film produced for ALA.

1978   Closure of the MLS program at the University of Oregon—followed by seventeen other closures by 2001.

Anglo-American Cataloging Rules, second edition (AACR2), is published.

1979   First White House Conference on Libraries.

Standards for university libraries are adopted by ACRL and ARL.

Stanford joins the Research Libraries Group, and the BALLOTS system is renamed the Research Library Information Network (RLIN).

OCLC implements an interlibrary loan system.

Public Library Mission Statement, new standards focus attention on goals and objectives.

1979   Kathleen Weibel and Kathleen M. Heim publish *The Role of Women in Librarianship, 1876–1976.* Updates continue this work.

Media Programs: District and School, new national standards for school library media centers, is released.

1980   *Planning Process for Public Libraries* is published. A shift from quantitative to qualitative standards for effective public library services.

F. Wilfred Lancaster's *The Impact of a Paperless Society on the Research Library of the Future* predicted a decline of artifacts, such as the book, as the primary vehicle for information storage and retrieval, and forecast that a paperless society will emerge, to be replaced by electronically accessible forms information.

1981   Publication of the *National Union Catalog, Pre-1956 Imprints* is completed in 754 volumes.

1982   *Output Measures for Public Libraries: A Manual of Standardized Procedures* is published.

James Thompson's *End of Libraries* predicts that computers will displace "mankind's book-centered communal memory."

The first Banned Books Week is observed.

ALA adopts updated statement on professional ethics.

1983   American Association of Library School's (AALS) changes its name to Association for Library and Information Science Education (ALISE).

1985   H. W. Wilson Co. makes *Reader's Guide to Periodical Literature, Library Literature Index,* and other indexes available in electronic format through Wilsonline.

The national library symbol adopted by ALA is approved for use by the Federal Highway Administration.

NSF created NSFNET, a series of networks used for research and education communication.

1986   The Library Book Fellows Program is inaugurated by ALA with a grant from USIA. Runs through 1998, allowing 100 U.S. librarians to participate in exchanges in 70 countries.

1987   *Planning and Role Setting for Public Libraries* is published as a self-help manual to help select among eight possible roles for public libraries.

First online journal appears (*New Horizons*—in adult education).

ALA and NCLIS launch a national campaign to sign up every child for a library card. The campaign theme is "The best gift you will ever give your child."

1988   *Information Power: Guidelines for School Library Media Programs* promotes the school library media specialist as a proactive initiator and participant in an instructional team.

ALA receives major grant from the DeWitt-Wallace/Reader's Digest Fund to coordinate the National Library Power Program based on the Information Power Guidelines.

Anglo-American Cataloging Rules, second edition, 1988 revision, is published (AACR2).

1989   The ALA Literacy Assembly is established—an example of ALA's continuing commitment to literacy and libraries.

1990   *Standards for Community, Junior, and Technical College Learning Resource Programs* is adopted.

Disabilities Act is approved with impact on libraries.

1991   OCLC launches PRISM, offering enhanced capabilities for online cataloging and searching. First end-user reference system in the library community.

High Performance Computing Act of 1991, NREN, is passed.

Second White House Conference on Library and Information Service.

1992   New accreditation standards for LIS education gives schools latitude in defining the scope and purpose of their master's degrees.

1994   First national study of public libraries and the Internet finds 20.9% connected. In 1997, 72% of public libraries have Internet connection. By the year 2002, it is 98.7%.

1995   "Vision ALA Goal 2000—Intellectual Participation" is adopted. As a five-year initiative, it envisioned that ALA would be identified as the voice of "intellectual participation." An ALA Office for Information Technology policy is also established.

1996   Federal library programs are moved from the Department of Education to the new Institute of Museum and Library Services.

Library Services and Technology Act is approved, an updated version of the LSCA with increased focus on information access through technology and on information empowerment.

Telecommunications Act of 1996 is passed by Congress.

Communications Decency Act is passed. Part of the above is challenged by ALA for violating the Constitution. Declared unconstitutional by Supreme Court in 1997.

1997   Microsoft founder Bill Gates and his wife, Melinda, establish the Gates Library Foundation (later the Bill and Melinda Gates Library Foundation) with a gift of $206 million to assist public libraries in providing Internet connections to the public.

Spectrum minority scholarships are offered by ALA as a four-year recruitment initiative.

1998   Digital Millennium Copyright Act of 1998 and Copyright Term Extension Act are approved.

Updated from 1988 is *Information Power: Building Partnership for Learning*, with a focus on information literacy in school library media centers.

1999   ALA convenes the first Congress on Professional Education; others follow yearly.

2000   The Children's Internet Protection Law (CIPA) is signed into law.

2001   ALA launches the @ Your Library campaign to foster a new understanding of the value of libraries to our democracy. USA Patriot Act is enacted, with a controversial impact on library records.

ALA files suit to prevent implementation of CIPA in public libraries.

2002   ALA establishes the ALA–Allied Professional Association to promote "the mutual professional interests of librarians, including certification."

2003   U.S. Supreme Court sides with CIPA.

2004   Google announces project to digitally scan books from the collections of five major research libraries and make them available online.

2005   ALA announces new strategic plan, "ALA Ahead to 2010."

Hurricane Katrina destroys and damages many libraries in Louisiana, Texas, and Mississippi.

Bibliography

The sources listed in this bibliography represent those used directly for the writing of this work as well as those that provided general information and background. Comments are made on some of the more important titles.

My brief review of what I called the "Golden Age of U.S. Librarianship, 1945–1970," published in 1984, provided a framework for the first half of the present work.

The most useful source to establish a chronology as well as the identification of events and developments was the *Bowker Annual*, which began publication in 1956. In almost every yearly edition, there was an article describing the highlights of library events during the previous year. Unfortunately, beginning in the early 1990s, these were usually limited to public and school library coverage. Professional journals would at times have special issues focusing on historical events such as *Library Journal*'s "Events of the Century." What would have been an excellent annual historical record ended publication in 1991. *The ALA Yearbook*, which began in 1976, was crammed with detailed information and commentary on each year's developments. An internal ALA document kept current by the executive director's office proved most valuable, *ALA Milestones—ALA Key Actions and Priority Areas, 1876–2004*, is a thirty-six-page, 11 × 17-inch tabular document showing "milestones" for each year under eleven headings: diversity, education and continuous learning, equity of access (access to information), intellectual freedom, literacy, legislation/funding, advocacy/public awareness, personnel resources, library services/development/technology, international relations, organization, and governance. Although limited to ALA, it is still useful because ALA was involved in almost every major library development from 1945 to the present.

For the chronologies of general history and technology, I used a wide assortment of historical encyclopedias, almanacs, and yearbooks.

For background information as well as detailed information on specific topics, the following were very valuable:

Encyclopedia of Library and Information Science (both editions)
Encyclopedia of Library History
International Dictionary of Library History
World Encyclopedia of Library and Information Services

The American Library Directory was invaluable for a historical review of the growth of library systems, networks, and consortia; state library agencies; schools of library and information science; and other organizations.

The Whole Library Handbook was valuable for the recent statistical data and for many nuggets of information over a wide range of topics.

Bruce Schuman's two books were useful for their review of major issues and trends from the 1940s to the 1990s.

Gregg Sapp's *Brief History of the Future of Libraries* was important for its historical review of previous predictions about the future of libraries.

There have been a number of autobiographies written recently by prominent librarians who were professionally active during most of the period under study. These provided important background and a flavor of the times. These are works by William R. Eshelman, David Kaser, and Paul Wasserman. To this list must also be added Ken Kister's biography of Eric Moon. Finally, one must add to this grouping three works by Herbert S. White. Although not biographical, they provide important personal commentary on many topics during the last four decades of the twentieth century.

Biographical sources used to identify the major leaders of the field have already been identified and described in chapter 9.

There were a number of recent books providing commentary about the current status of libraries as well as about their past and future. They often provided a unique perspective and new insights. They were helpful in the formulation of some of my own evaluative comments and conclusions. I refer to Nicholas Basbane's *Patience and Fortitude*, Peter Brophy's *The Library in the Twenty-first Century*, Walt Crawford and Michael Gorman's *Future of Libraries*, and Michael Gorman's *The Enduring Library*.

The websites of the National Center for Educational Statistics and the Association of Research Libraries provided much useful statistical data.

Finally, there were people as information resources. Many of these are listed in the acknowledgments. Professional colleagues were very generous in responding to e-mail and telephone inquiries with facts, opinions, referrals to other sources of information, and copies of various documents.

REFERENCES

ALA Milestones—ALA Key Actions and Priority Areas, 1876–2004.
An internally produced checklist kept up on a continuing basis by the ALA executive director's office.

The ALA Yearbook, 1976–1983. Chicago: American Library Association, 1976–1983.

The ALA Yearbook of Library and Information Services, 1984–1990. Chicago: American Library Association, 1984–1990.

The American Library Association Celebrates 50 Years of Presence and Service by Its Washington Office: Honoring Legislative and Grass Roots Library Champions, May 6, 1996. Washington, D.C.: American Library Association Washington Office, 1996.

American Library Directory: A Classified List of Libraries in the United States and Canada, with Personnel and Statistical Data. New York: R. R. Bowker, 1923–.

Baker, Nicholson. *Double Fold: Libraries and the Assault on Paper.* New York: Random House, 2001.

Basbanes, Nicholas A. *Patience and Fortitude: A Roving Chronicle of Book People, Book Places, and Book Culture.* New York: Harper Collins, 2001.

"Bill Gates: Why He Did It," *American Libraries* 43 (December 2003): 48–56.

Bobinski, George S. "The Golden Age of U.S. Librarianship, 1945–1970." *Wilson Library Bulletin* 53 (January 1984): 338–44.

Bobinski, George S., Jesse Hauk Shera, and Bohdan W. Wynar, eds. *Dictionary of American Library Biography.* Littleton, Colo.: Libraries Unlimited, 1978.
Supplement, edited by Wayne A. Wiegand, 1990.
Second supplement, edited by Donald G. Davis, Jr., 2003.

"Books, Bricks, and Bytes" *Daedalus* (Fall 1996).
Special issue celebrating the New York Public Library Centennial.

Bowker Annual of Library and Booktrade Information. New York: Bowker, 1956–.

Brophy, Peter. *The Library in the Twenty-first Century: New Service for the Information Age.* London: Library Association, 2001.

Buckland, Michael K., and Trudy Hahn, eds. "History of Documentation and Information Science." Special issue, pts. 1 and 2. *JASIS* 48 (April 1997); (September 1997).

Carroll, Francis Laverne, and Joan Frederick Harvey. *International Librarianship: Cooperation and Collaboration.* Lanham, Md.: Scarecrow Press, 2001.

Case, Donald. *Looking for Information: A Survey of Research on Information Seeking, Need and Behavior.* San Diego, Calif.: Academic Press, 2002.

Council on Library Resources Annual Reports. Washington, D.C.: Council on Library and Information Resources, 1957–.
Name changed to Council on Library and Information Resources in 1996.

Council on Library Resources. "The Council on Library Resources: Shaping a Foundation for the Future." Washington, D.C.: Council on Library Resources, 1993.
A special insert by Robert Gurwitt to the 1993 CLR Annual Report.

Cox, Richard J. "America's Pyramids: Presidents and Their Libraries." *Government Information Quarterly* 19 (2003): 45–75.

———. *Vandals in the Stacks: A Response to Nicholson Baker's Assault on Libraries.* Westport, Conn.: Greenwood Press, 2002.

Crawford, Walt, and Michael Gorman. *Future of Libraries: Dreams, Madness and Reality.* Chicago: American Library Association, 1995.

Darling, Pamela. "From Problems Perceived to Programs in Practice: The Preservation of Library Resources in the USA, 1956–1980." *Library Resources and Technical Services* 25 (January–March 1981): 9–29.

Dawson, Alma. "Celebrating African-American Librarians and Librarianship." *Library Trends* 49 (Summer 2000): 49–87.

Downs, Robert B. *A Dictionary of Eminent Librarians.* Worland, Wyo.: High Plains, 1990.

DuMont, Rosemary Ruhig, Lois Buttlar, and William Canyon. *Multiculturalism in Libraries.* Westport, Conn.: Greenwood Press, 1994.

Encyclopedia of Library and Information Science. 72 vols. New York: Marcel Dekker, 1968–2002.
Second edition, 4 vols. 2003.

Eshelman, William R. *No Silence! A Library Life.* Lanham, Md.: Scarecrow Press, 1997.

"Events of the Century." *Library Journal* 124 (December 1999): 74–75.

Farber, Evan. "College Libraries and the Teaching/Learning Process: A 25-Year Reflection." *Journal of Academic Librarianship* 25 (May 1999): 171–77.

Fourie, Denise K., and David R. Dowell. *Librarians in the Information Age: An Information and Career Exploration* Greenwood, Colo.: Libraries Unlimited, 2002.

Freeman, Robert, and David M. Hovde, eds. *Libraries to the People: Histories of Outreach* Jefferson, N.C.: McFarland, 2003.

Gordon, Andrew, et al. "The Gates Legacy." *Library Journal* 128 (March 1, 2003): 44–47.

Gorman, Michael. *The Enduring Library: Technology, Tradition and the Quest for Balance.* Chicago: American Library Association, 2003.

Grassian, Esther. "Building on Bibliographic Instruction." *American Libraries* 35 (October 2004): 51–53.

Hahn, Trudi Bellardo, and Michael Buckland, eds. *Historical Studies in Information Sciences* Medford, N.J.: Information Today, 1998.

Hannigan, Matthew. "What a Long Strange Trip It's Been: The History of Online Searching." *Indiana Libraries* 18 (2000): 2–11. Suppl. no. 2.

Hardesty, Larry L. "Reflections on 25 Years of Library Instruction: Have We Made Progress?" *Reference Services Review* 27 (1999): 242–46.

"Highlights from LJ's 120 Years." *Library Journal* 121 (July 1996): 57–69.

Hildenbrand, Suzanne. "Library Feminism and Library Women's History: Activism and Scholarship, Equity and Culture." *Libraries and Culture* 35 (Winter 2000): 51–65.

Hood, Joan M. "Past, Present, and Future of Library Development (Fund Raising)." *Advances in Librarianship* 22 (1998): 123–39.

Horrocks, Norman, ed. *Perspectives, Insights and Priorities: 17 Leaders Speak Freely of Librarianship.* Lanham, Md.: Scarecrow Press, 2005.

James, Joseph. *Introduction to Reference Work in the Digital Age.* New York: Neal-Schuman, 2003.

Josey, E. J. *Black Librarian in America.* Lanham, Md.: Scarecrow Press, 1970.

Josey, E. J., and Marla L. DeLoach, eds. *Handbook of Black Librarianship.* 2nd ed. Lanham, Md.: Scarecrow Press, 2000.
    See also the first edition, published in 1977.

Journal of Academic Librarianship 25, nos. 1–6 (1994).
    Twenty-fifth anniversary volume.

Kaser, David. *Just Lucky, I Guess.* New York: Vantage, 2000.

Katz, William. *Cuneiform to Computer: A History of Reference Sources.* Lanham, Md.: Scarecrow Press, 1990.

Kister, Kenneth F. *Eric Moon: The Life and Times.* Jefferson, N.C.: McFarland, 2002.

"Knowledge Services and SLA's History: An Interview with Guy St. Clair." *Information Outlook* 7 (September 2003): 16–19.

Krug, Judith F. "ALA and Intellectual Freedom: An Historical Overview" In *Intellectual Freedom Manual.* 6th ed., 3–32. Chicago: American Library Association, 2002.

Lancaster, F. W. "Second Thoughts on the Paperless Society." *Library Journal* 124 (September 15, 1999): 48–50.

Levinson, Paul. *Soft Edge: A Natural History and Future of the Information Revolution.* London: Routledge, 1997.

Libraries and Information Services Today. Chicago: American Library Association, 1991.

Library and Information Science Education Statistical Report, 1983 to date. Oak Ridge, Tenn.: Association of Library and Information Science Education, 1983–.

Logan, Elisabeth, and Ingrid Hsieh-Yee. "Library and Information Science Education in the Nineties." *Annual Review of Information Science and Technology* 35 (2001): 425–77.

Long, Sarah Ann Sanders. "Systems, Quo Vadis? An Examination of the History, Current Status, and Nature of Regional Library Systems." *Advances in Librarianship* 19 (1999): 117–68.

Lorenzen, Michael. "A Brief History of Library Information in the United States of America." *Illinois Libraries* 83 (Spring 2001): 8–18.

Markey, Karen. "Current Educational Trends in the Information and Library Science Curriculum." *Journal Education for Library and Information Science* 45 (Fall 2004): 317–39.

Martin, Lowell. *Enrichment: A History of the Public Library in the United States in the Twentieth Century.* Lanham, Md.: Scarecrow Press, 1998.

McCrank, Lawrence J. *Historical Information Science: An Emerging Undiscipline.* Medford, N.J.: Information Today, 2001.

Michie, Joan, and Barbara A. Holton. *Fifty Years of Supporting Children's Learning: A History of Public School Libraries and Federal Legislation from 1953–2000.* Washington, D.C.: National Center for Education Statistics, 2005.

Miller, Ruth H. "Electronic Resources in Academic Libraries, 1980–2000: A Historical Perspective." *Library Trends* 48 (Spring 2000): 645–70.

Molz, Kathleen. *Civic Space/Cyberspace: The American Public Library in the Information Age* Cambridge, Mass.: MIT Press, 1999.

Morris, Betty J. *Administering the School Library Media Center.* New Providence, N.J.: Bowker, 1992.

Mount, Ellis. *Special Libraries and Information Centers: An Introductory Text.* Washington, D.C.: Special Libraries Association, 1999.

"100 of the Most Important Leaders We Had." *American Libraries* 30 (December 1999): 38–47.

Powell, Ronald R. "Trends and Issues in Academic Libraries." *Journal of Education for Library and Information Science* 42 (Winter 2001): 69–71.

Rosencheck, Donna. "OCLC: From an Historical Perspective." *Katharine Sharp Review* 4 (Winter 1997).

Sager, Don. "Before the Memory Fades: Public Libraries in the Twentieth Century." *Public Libraries* 39 (March–April 2000): 73–77.

Salony, Mary F. "The History of Bibliographic Instruction: Changing Trend from Books to the Electronic World." *Reference Librarian,* no. 51–52 (1995): 31–61.

Sapp, Gregg. *A Brief History of the Future of Libraries.* Lanham, Md.: Scarecrow Press, 2002.

Shuman, Bruce. *Issues for Libraries and Information Science in the Internet Age.* Englewood, Colo.: Libraries Unlimited, 2001.

Shuman, Bruce, with Carole J. McCollough and Joseph Mika. *Foundations and Issues in Library and Information Science.* Englewood, Colo.: Libraries Unlimited, 1992.

Smith, K. Wayne. "OCLC: Yesterday, Today and Tomorrow." *Journal of Library Administration* 26 (November 1998): 251–70.

Stam, Dave H. *International Dictionary of Library History.* Chicago: Fitzroy, 2001.

Straw, Joseph E. "From Magicians to Teachers: The Development of Electronic Reference in Libraries: 1930–2000." *Reference Librarian,* no 74 (2001): 1–12.

Tolzmann, Don Heinrich, Alfred Hessland, and Reuben Price. *The Memory of Mankind: The Story of Libraries since the Dawn of Time.* New Castle, Del.: Oak Knoll Press, 2001.

Wasserman, Paul. *The Best of Times: A Personal and Occupational Odyssey.* Detroit, MI: Omnigraphics, 2000.

Webb, T. D., ed. *Building Libraries for the 21st Century: The Shape of Information.* Jefferson, N.C.: McFarland, 2000.

Weibel, Kathleen, and Kathleen M. Heim, with Dianne J. Ellsworth, eds. *Role of Women in Librarianship, 1876–1976: The Entry, Advancement and Struggles for Equalization in One Profession.* Phoenix, AZ: Oryx, 1979.
Updated in *One Account of Sex: An Annotated Bibliography on the Status of Women,* by various authors, 1981, 1984, 1989, 1993, 2000.

White, Herbert S. *At the Crossroads: Libraries on the Information Superhighway.* Englewood, Colo.: Libraries Unlimited, 1995.

———. *Librarians and the Awakening from Innocence: A Collection of Papers.* Boston: C. K. Hall, 1989.

———. *Librarianship—Quo Vadis: Opportunities and Dangers as We Face the New Millennium.* Englewood, Colo.: Libraries Unlimited, 2000.

The Whole Library Handbook, compiled by George M. Eberhart. Chicago: American Library Association, 1991.

The Whole Library Handbook—2, 1995.

The Whole Library Handbook—3, 2000.

Wiegand, Wayne A., and Donald G. Davis, Jr., eds. *Encyclopedia of Library History.* New York: Garland, 1994.

Williams, R. V. "The Documentation and Special Library Movement in the U.S., 1910–1960." *JASIS* 48 (September 1997): 775–81.

Wilson, Anthony M., and Robert Hermanson. "Educating and Training Library Practitioners: A Comparative History with Trends and Recommendations." *Library Trends* 46 (Winter 1998): 469–504.

Woolls, Blanche. *The School Library Media Manager.* 2nd ed. Englewood, Colo.: Libraries Unlimited, 1990.

World Encyclopedia of Library and Information Services. 3rd ed. Chicago: American Library Association, 1993.

The Yearly Chronicle, 1991. Chicago: American Library Association, 1991.

AACR. *See The Anglo-American Cataloging Rules*

AACR2. *See The Anglo-American Cataloging Rules,* second edition

AALS. *See* Association of American Library Schools

AASL. *See* American Association of School Librarians

AASL Distinguished Service Award, 130

AAUP. *See* American Association of University Professors; Association of University Professors

abstracting services, 15

Academic Facilities Act (1963), 42, 68, 165

Academic Library Advancement and Development Network (ALADN), 74

Academic Library Management Intern Program, 78

Academic Press, 46

Access to Public Libraries (ALA), 98

An Account of Sex: An Annotated Bibliography on the Status of Women in Librarianship, 96

accreditation, MLS, 48, 84, 114–18, *117,* 122–24, 133, 150, 164, 168

ACLU. *See* American Civil Liberties Union

acquisitions, expenditures for, 7, *11,* 50

ACRL. *See* Association of College and Research Libraries

ACRL Academic/Research Librarian of the Year Award, 130

ADI. *See* American Society for Information Science

Adult Education Act (1966), 31

Adult Education Activities in Public Libraries (Lyman), 30–31

Adult Services in the Eighties (McCook), 32

Advance Research Project Agency (ARPA), 167

AECT, 39, 170, 171

African Americans, library service and, 97–100, 151–52

agencies, state library, 5, 27

Agricultural Trade Development and Assistance Act (1954), 50

Airlie House Conference, 115, 119

ALA. *See* American Library Association

ALA Ahead to 2010, 87, 172

ALA–Allied Professional Association (ALA–APA), 86, 172

ALA–APA. *See* ALA–Allied Professional Association

A.L.A. Cataloguing Rules for Authors and Title Entries, 12, 164. *See also* cataloging

ALADN. *See* Academic Library Advancement and Development Network

ALA Equity Award, 96

ALA Honorary Membership, 129

ALA Library Community Project, 31, 72

ALA Round Table. *See* Library Instruction Round Table

ALD. *See American Library Directory*

ALISE. *See* Association for Library and Information Science Education

Allain, Alex P., 131–32

Allied Professional Association (ALA), 124

Americana (DeLitto), 90

American Association of School Librarians (AASL), 37, 39, 93

American Association of State Libraries, 56

American Association of University Professors (AAUP), 42, 164

American Book Center, 92

American Civil Liberties Union (ACLU), 91

American Documentation Institute (ADI). *See* American Society for Information Science

American Heritage Discussion Series, 72

American Heritage Project, 30

American Indian Association, 101

American Libraries, 117, 130

American Libraries Association: Spectrum Initiative for, 102, 172

American Library Association (ALA): *Access to Public Libraries* by, 98; accreditation by, 48, 84, 114–18, *117,* 122–24, 133, 150, 164, 168; ACRL by, 45; *Adult Education Activities in Public Libraries* (Lyman), 30–31; ALA Ahead to 2010 for, 87, 172; "@ Your Library" by, 85, 86; awards through, 129–31; Black Caucus for, 85, 168; Board on International Relations by, 91–92; *Books for College Libraries* by, 77, 167; Campaign for American Libraries for, 74; Carnegie Corporation support for, 9, 74–75; *Choice* by, 45, 77, 165; CLR assistance to, 77; Committee on Accreditation for, 168; Committee on Preservation of Library Materials for, 106; controversy within, 86; *Cost Funding for Public Libraries* by, 28; Council for, 19; development of, 84–85; Development Office for Fundraising for, 74; *Directions for Library Service to Young Adults* by, 33, 169; discussion lists for, 84; diversity within, 2, 5, 97–102, 151–52; Film Advisory Service for, 9; Freedom to Read Foundation by, 89–90, 150–51, 168; Fund for Adult Education for, 72; *Guidelines for Audiovisual Materials and Services for Public Libraries* for, 27; *Guidelines for Library Service in Healthcare Institutions* by, 168; IFC by, 87; intellectual freedom and, 87–89, 150–51; Intellectual Freedom Committee for, 87, 89; Knapp School Libraries Project by, 37–38, 72, 165–66; librarian exchange through, 94; Library-21 exhibit by, 20, 85, 165; Library Bill of Rights by, 87–88, 90, 98, 100, 150; Library Book Fellows Program by, 170; Library Community Project by, 31, 72; "Library Education and Manpower" by, 115; Library Instruction Round Table for, 47; Literacy Assembly of, 86, 171; lobbying by, 38, 150; *Minimum Standards for Public Library Systems,* 27, 167; *National Inventory of Library Needs* by, 116; National Legislative Day by, 85, 168; National Library Power Program by, 171; *New Directions in Library and Information Science Education* by, 121; *New Planning for Results* by, 29; Office for Diversity for, 2, 5, 97–102, 151–52; Office for Intellectual Freedom for, 89, 150–51, 167; Office for Library Education for, 115; Office for Literacy and Outreach Services for, 85; *Output Measures for Public Libraries* by, 28; *Output Measures for Public Library Services to Children: A Manual of Standardized Procedures* by, 29; *Planning and Role Setting for Public Libraries* by, 28–29, 170; Planning Committee for, 97–98; *Planning for Results: A Public Library Transformation Process* by, 29; *Planning Process for Public Libraries* by, 28, 169; policy/directives by, 32, 88, 92, 102, 115; "Policy on Confidentiality of Library Records" by, 88–89; preservation by, 106, 107, 152; Preservation Policy for, 107; publications by, 77, 85–86, 98; *Public Library Mission Statement* by, 27–28, 169; *Public Library Plans for the Teen Age* by, 33; *Public Library Service: A Guide to Evaluation* by, 27, 165; role of, 84; *School Libraries for Today and Tomorrow: Functions and Standards* by, 37, 163; Social Responsibilities Round Table for, 85, 168; Social Science Research Council study for, 27; *Standards for Children's Services in Public Libraries* for, 27, 166; *Standards for Work with Young Adults,* 27, 165; Task Force on the Status of Women by, 96, 168; Task Force on Women for, 85; "Vision ALA Goal 2000—Intellectual Participation " by, 171; Young Adult Library Services Association for, 74; *Young Adult Services in the Public Library* by, 33

American Library Directory (ALD), 2, 50, *52,* 64, 65, 148

American Society for Information Science, 51, 115, 119, 167

Ameritech, 73

Andrew Carnegie Medals of Philanthropy, 75

And Something More (Knapp School Libraries Project), 38

Angel Network Book Club, 74. *See also* Winfrey, Oprah

The Anglo-American Cataloging Rules (CLR), 12, 78, 167. *See also* cataloging

The Anglo-American Cataloging Rules, second edition (CLR), 13–14, 78, 169, 171

Annual Congress on Professional Change (ALA), 86

Annual Review of Information Science and Technology, 119

Appalachian Regional Development, 69

Apple computers, 4, 163

Arbuthnot, May H., 132

ARL. *See* Association of Research Libraries

ARPA. *See* Advance Research Project Agency

ARPANET, 167

art reproductions, 10

Asheim, Lester E., 115, 132

Asian Americans, library service and, 32, 83, 101, 102, 152

Asian/Pacific American Librarians Association, 101

Association for Library and Information Science Education (ALISE), 96–97, 120, 170

Association for Library Collections and Technical Services, 106

Association for Library Service to Children's ALSC Distinguished Service Award, 130

Association of American Library Schools (AALS), 119–20, 170

Association of College and Research Libraries (ACRL), 42, 44, 45, 46, 78, 86

Association of Research Libraries (ARL), 41, 43–44, 74–75, 97, 107, 109

Association of School Librarians, 86

Association of University Professors (AAUP), 153

associations, professional librarian, 2, 5, 81–87, *82, 83, 84,* 150. *See also* American Library Association; individual association names

Astor Foundation, 73

AT&T, 73

"@ Your Library" (ALA), 85, 86

audiovisual materials. *See* technology

Avram, Henriette, 12, 129, 132–33

awards, for librarianship, 129–31

Bachelor of Library Science (BLS), 2, 113–14, 126

Baker, Augusta, 133

Baker, Nicholson, 108–9

Baker, Shirley K., 109

BALLOTS. *See* Bibliographic Automation of Large Library Operations Using a Time-Sharing Unit System

Banks, Paul, 106

Banned Books Week, 170

Barrow, William J., 79

Basart, Ann, 146

Batchelder, Mildred L., 131

Baylor University Fine Arts Library, 22

Beheshti, J., 121–22

Bell Atlantic, 73

Bender, David, 144

Benton Foundation, 36

Benton, Rita, 146

Berman, Sanford, 133

Berring, Robert, 145

Beta Phi Mu, 82, *83,* 93, 114

Beta Phi Mu Award, 129, 130

Bete, Channing, Sr., 69–70

BI. *See* bibliographic instruction

Bibliographic Automation of Large Library Operations Using a Time-Sharing Unit System (BALLOTS), 13, 43, 60, 77, 167, 168. *See also* Research Library Information Network

bibliographic instruction (BI), 14, 46–48

Bibliographic Instruction Section (ACRL), 47

Bibliographic Service Development Program (BSDP), 78

Bidlack, Russell E., 133–34

The Big Book of Library Grant Money 2006 (Taft), 76

Bill and Melinda Gates Foundation, 75–76, 129, 172

Billington, James H., 50

Black Librarian in America (Josey), 99

blogging. *See* technology

Bloomquist, Harold, 145

BLS. *See* Bachelor of Library Science

Board on International Relations (ALA), 91–92

books: acid-free paper for, 107; costs of, 26; demand *v.* supply of, 29–30; as electronic, 11, 153–54, 172; electronic resources *v.,* 7; for library science, 2; paperbacks as, 3; preservation of, 5, 55, 79, 105–11, 152, 168; in print, *8;* publication of, 2, 4, 7, 8, *8,* 46–47

Books for College Libraries (ALA), 77, 167

Books in Print, 2

Boorstin, Daniel J., 50, 73

Bowker Annual of Library and Book Trade Information (Bowker), 53, 104, 125–26

Bowker, R.R., 39, 53, 104, 125–26, 130, 156

Bradley, Carol June, 146

Brandon, Alfred, 145

Brittle Books (CLR), 79, 107

Brittle Books Program, 108

Brodman, Estelle, 145

Brown v. Louisiana, 99

BRS database, 15, 21

BSDP. *See* Bibliographic Service Development Program

Buddington, William, 144

buildings, library, 4, 5, 23, 103–5, *104*

Bush, George H. W., 55

Bush, George W., 39–40

Bush, Laura, 40

Bush, Vannevar, 15

Campaign for American Libraries (ALA), 74

Campbell, Frank C., 146

Canadian Library Association (CLA), 93
card catalog, end of, 13, 21
Carnegie Corporation, 9, 25, 27, 29, 72, 74–75, 80, 103, 164
Carnovsky, Leon, 134
Carter, Jimmy, 55
cataloging: *The Anglo-American Cataloging Rules* for, 12; *The Anglo-American Cataloging Rules*, second edition for, 13; demand for, 12; by librarians, 13; MARC for, 12, 13–14, 21, 43, 60, 62, 78, 129, 148, 149, 158, 166; *National Union Catalog of Pre-1956 Imprints* for, 12, 167, 170; PRISM for, 13, 171; redundancy in, 12; *Rules for Descriptive Cataloguing in the Library of Congress,* 12, 164
Cataloging in Publication (CIP), 12, 168
catalogs, online. *See* online public access catalogs; technology
CDA. *See* Communications Decency Act
CD-ROM technology, 10, 16, 17, 21, 30
censorship, 87–88, 170
Center for Documentation and Communication Research, 114, 142, 164
Center for Research Libraries, 41, 59–60, 61
Center for the Book. *See* Library of Congress
certification, librarians', 27, 31, 40, 86
Cheney, Francis N., 134
Child Online Protection Act (COPA), 91

Children's Internet Protection Act (CIPA), 91, 150, 172
Chinese American Librarians Association, 101
Choice (ALA), 45, 77, 165
CIP. *See* Cataloging in Publication
CIPA. *See* Children's Internet Protection Act
circulation, library, 4, 10, 26, 34, *35*
Civil Rights Act (1964), 3, 162
civil rights movement, 3, 97–100, 162
CLA. *See* Canadian Library Association
Clapp, Verner W., 77, 134
Clift, David H., 85, 134–35
Clinton, William, 55, 70, 90
CLIR. *See* Council on Library and Information Resources
CLR. *See* Council on Library Resources
CLSI, 169
Cohen, Morris, 145
Colaianni, Lois Ann, 145
Colby, Edward E., 146
Cold War, 3
Cole, Bruce, 110
Cole, Fred, 77
collections, library: access *v.* ownership, 10, 19–20, 44, 153–54; books for, 2; composition of, 2; development of, 29–30; as digital, 4, 10–11, 22, 44, 107–8, 153–54; management policy for, 7; preservation of, 5, 55, 79, 105–11, 152, 168; through public libraries, 23; for reference, 14; reference service for, 4, 5, 10, 14–16, 17, 19, 21, 23, 145,

153–54, 167; special personnel for, 14, *19*; for special purpose, 9

collective bargaining, 18

"College Libraries Director Mentor Program" (CLR), 78

Commission on Preservation and Access (CLR), 79, 107

Committee on Accreditation (ALA), 168

Committee on Preservation of Library Materials (ALA), 106

Communications Decency Act (CDA), 90–91, 171

communication technology, 4, 12, 14

community colleges, 41

"Competencies for Information Professionals of the 21st Century," 53–54

"Competencies for Special Librarians of the 21st Century" (SLA), 52. *See also* "Competencies for Information Professionals of the 21st Century"

computers: by Apple, 4, 163; databases on, 15; by IBM, 4, 16; for information control, 15; Internet Explorer for, 4, 16, 19, 21, 163; in libraries, 2, 4, 19, 26, 44; Macintosh as, 4; Mosaic for, 4, 16; Navigator for, 4, 16; online information services through, 4, 13, 15, 17, 19, 21, 26, 43, 153–54; for reference service, 14; Windows for, 4

Congress on Professional Education (ALA), 124, 172

CONSER. *See* Conversion of Serials program

conservation, of library materials, 5

consortia: library cooperation through, 5, 12, 19, 21, 27, 31, 38–39, 43, 45–46, 149–50; for New York, 65; WNYLRC as, 64–65

Conversion of Serials program (CONSER), 78

Cooke, Eileen, 135

Coover, James B., 146

COPA. *See* Child Online Protection Act

copiers, in libraries, 2

Copyright Act (1976), 169

Copyright Term Extension Act, 172

Cost Funding for Public Libraries (ALA), 28

Council on Library and Information Resources (CLIR), 5, 67, 72, 76–80, 107, 109, 149

Council on Library Resources (CLR), 20, 37, 45, 72, 107, 164, 165. *See also* Council on Library and Information Resources

Council on Library Technical Assistants, 114–15. *See also* Media Technical Assistants

Crisman, Linda, 86

Cuneiform Digital Library Initiative, 22

Cunha, George D. M., 106, 135

Cunningham, Virginia, 146

Current List of Medical Literature (NLM), 78. *See also Index Medicus;* MEDLARS

"Curriculum Guidelines for the School Library Media Specialist Program" (ALA/AASL), 123

curriculum, MLS, 120–22, 123, 152, 164

DALB. *See Dictionary of American Library Biography*
Dalton, Jack, 135
Daniel J. and Ruth F. Boorstin Publication Fund, 73
Danner, Richard, 145
Darling, Louise, 145
databases, computer: access to, 26, 153–54; audience for, 15; BRS as, 15, 21; CD-ROM for, 10, 16, 17, 21; DIALOG as, 15, 21, 163; INFOBANK as, 163; by LC, 78; for national sharing, 78; ORBIT as, 15, 163; simultaneous use of, 15. *See also* technology
data, migration of, 111
DAVI. *See* Department of Audio Visual Instruction of the National Education Association
"Deadline: The Author's Bid to Save America's Past" (Baker), 108
DeLitto, Don, 90
Denver Public Library, 26. *See also* libraries, public
Department of Audio Visual Instruction of the National Education Association (DAVI), 38
Depository Act (1962), 68
desktop publishing. *See* technology
Development Office for Fundraising (ALA), 74
Development Officers of Research Academic Libraries, North America (Doral, NA), 74
Dewey Medal, 129
Dewey, Melvil, 129
DeWitt-Wallace/Reader's Digest Foundation, 39, 170
DIALOG database, 15, 21, 163

Dictionary of American Library Biography (DALB), 126, 130
digital backup files. *See* technology
Digital Electronics Corporation, 169
Digital Library Federation, 79, 107
Digital Library Program, 50, 73
Digital Millennium Copyright Act (1998), 172
Directions for Library Service to Young Adults (ALA), 33, 169
Directory of Special Libraries and Information Centers, 51
Disabilities Act, 171
discussion lists, 84. *See also* Internet
Dixon, William S., 135–36
documentalists, 51
Doral, N. A. *See* Development Officers of Research Academic Libraries, North America
Double Fold: Libraries and the Assault on Paper (Baker), 108
Dougherty, Richard M., 136
Downs, Robert B., 136
Drey, Thomas R., Jr., 73

Earlham College Library, 47
e-books. *See* books; technology
Economic Opportunity Act, 69
education, American, 3, 4, 5, 9, 54
education, library and information science, 5, 6, 69, 82–84, 96–97, 113–25, *116, 117, 118,* 119, 126–27, 152–53, 170, 171
education, library user, 46–48
Edwards, Margaret, 136
Eisenhower, Dwight D., 49, 54–55, 165
electronic resources, 7, 20. *See also* technology

Elementary and Secondary Education Act (ESEA), 38, 68–69, 166

Eli M. Obler Award, 90

Ellsworth, Ralph E., 136–37

e-mail, 16, 19, 21. *See also* Internet; libraries; technology

Encyclopedia of Library and Information Science, 126, 156

The End of Libraries (Thompson), 156, 170

Equal Rights Amendments, 96

ESEA. *See* Elementary and Secondary Education Act

Evans, Luther H., 49

facsimiles. *See* technology

Faculty/Librarian Cooperative Research Program, 78

Faculty Status for Academic Libraries (ACRL), 42

Farber, Evan, 47

Farmington Plan, 41, 164

FBI. *See* Federal Bureau of Investigation

Federal Bureau of Investigation (FBI), 88–89

Federal Highway Administration, 85, 170

Fellowship Program (CLR), 78

The Feminine Mystique (Friedan), 3, 95, 162

feminism, 3, 95–96, 162. *See also* women

Ferguson, Elizabeth, 144

Film Advisory Service, 9

film, evolution of. *See* technology

Finley, Elizabeth, 145

FirstSearch, 16. *See also* Ohio College Library Center

Fogarty, John E., 137

Folger Library, 77

Ford, Barbara, 92

Ford Foundation, 72, 76, 77, 79

Ford, Gerald R., 50, 55

Foundation Center, 71, 74

freedom, intellectual, 5, 81, 87–89, 90, 150–51, 167

Freedom Libraries, 98

Freedom of Information Act, 89

Freedom to Read Foundation (ALA), 89–90, 150–51, 168

Friedan, Betty, 3, 95, 162

Friends of the Library USA, 76

Frye Leadership Institute, 79

Fulbright Program, 93–94

Fund for Adult Education, 72

funding, library federal, 2, 5, 9, 25–26, 27, 31, 38, 42, 67–71, 149

Gallagher, Marian, 145

Gasaway, Laura, 145

Gates, Bill, 75–76, 129, 137, 172

Gates Program, 75–76, 129, 172

Gaver, Mary, 137

gender, of librarians, 2, 5, 18, 43, 95–97

GI Bill, 3

Gibson, Robert W., Jr., 144

Gonzalez, Robert W., 145

Google, 11, 172. *See also* Internet; technology

Gorman, Michael, 137–38

governments, state, 27, 30–31, 55–57

The Grapes of Wrath (Steinbeck), 87

Great Books Foundation, 30, 72

Great Issues program, 30

Great Society's War on Poverty, 3, 31. *See also* Johnson, Lyndon B.

Guidelines for Audiovisual Materials and Services for Public Libraries (ALA), 27

Guidelines for Library Service in Healthcare Institutions (ALA), 168

Guidelines for Two-year College and Learning Resources Program, 41–42, 165

Guidelines for Young Adult Services in Public Libraries, 167

The Gutenberg Galaxy (McLuhan), 156, 165

Handbook of Black Librarianship (Josey), 99–100

Harvard University, 11, 41, 43, 60, 63, 141, *148,* 157

Heim, Kathleen M., 96, 169

Henne, Frances W., 138

Hewitt, Vivian D., 100

Heyer, Anna H., 146

Higher Education Act (1965), 42, 68, 115, 124, 166

High Performance Computing Act (1991) (NREN), 171

Hill, Richard S., 146

Hispanics, library service and, 24, 62, 83, 100–101, 102, 152

A History of the American Library Association (Thomison), 85–86

Holley, Edward G., 138

homeless, public libraries and, 24

Hooker, Ruth, 145

Hoover, Herbert, 55

Houder, Frank, 145

Humphrey, James, III, 145

Hurricane Katrina, 72, 172

H. W. Wilson Foundation, 72–73, 115, 170

IBM. *See* International Business Machines

IFC. *See* Intellectual Freedom Committee

IFLA. *See* International Federation of Library Associations

IFRT. *See* Intellectual Freedom Round Table

IL. *See* information literacy

immigration/migration, 3, 24, 33

The Impact of the Paperless Society on Research Libraries of the Future (Lancaster), 156, 170

Index Medicus, 15, 78. *See also* National Library of Medicine

Index of American Public Library Circulation, 34, *35*

inflation, 25

INFOBANK database, 163

information: access to, 4, 19–20, 153–54; CD-ROM technology for, 10, 16, 17, 21; explosion in, 3, 7, 41, 60, 148; through Internet, 4, 10, 16, 17, 19, 21

Information and Referral centers (I&R), 14

information highway, 26, 153–54

information literacy (IL), 46–48

Information Outlook, 52

Information Power: Building Partnerships for Learning, 39, 172

Information Power: Guidelines for School Library Media Programs (AALS/AECT), 39, 170, 171

information professional (IP), 53

information science, 119

information technology, 7

Informed Librarian Online, 126

Institute of Museum and Library Service, 71, 171

instruction, library, 14
Intellectual Freedom Committee
    (IFC), 87, 89
Intellectual Freedom Round Table
    (IFRT), 90, 150–51
intellectuals, distrust of, 3
intelligence, artificial, 21
International Association of School
    Librarians, 93
International Business Machines
    (IBM), 4, 16
International Federation of Library
    Associations (IFLA), 92, 100
International Relations Round Table,
    92, 94
Internet, 4, 10, 16, 17, 19, 21, 36,
    44, 48, 84, 91, 110–11, 148, 150,
    154, 158, 171, 172
Internet Archive Project, 110–11
Internet Explorer, 4, 16, 19, 21, 163
Internet Public Library, 36
Introduction to Reference Work
    (Katz), 167
Iowa State Library, 30
IP. *See* information professional
iPods. *See* technology
I&R. *See* Information and Referral
    centers
Isadore Gilbert Mudge-R.R. Bowker
    Award, 130
ISBN. *See* Standard Book Number
ISSN, 12. *See also* serials
Italian American Librarian Caucus,
    101

Jackson, Eugene B., 145
Javits, Jacob, 70
Jewish Librarians Task Force, 101
John Phillip Immroth Memorial
    Award for Intellectual Freedom, 90

Johnson, Lyndon B., 31, 55, 68, 69,
    167
Jones, Clara S., 85, 100
Jones, Jerry, 73
Jones, Virginia L., 138
Josey, E. J., 99–100, 139
*Journal for Library and Information
    Science Education,* 114
*Journal of Education for
    Librarianship,* 114, 165.
    *See also Journal for Library
    and Information Science
    Education*
journals, professional, 2, 8, 11, 39,
    45, 47, 97, 105, 114, 115, 117,
    126, 165, 169. *See also* individual
    titles
JSTOR, 46, 93

Kahn, Edmund/Louis Uraff, 73
Katherine Sharpe Review, 126
Katz, William A., 167
Kellogg-Alise Information
    Professions and Education
    Reform Project, 122
Kennedy, John F., 55, 162
Kenney, Anne R., 110
Kilgour, Fred, 12, 42, 61, 129, 139,
    167
Knapp Foundation, 37–38, 72
Knapp, Patricia, 47
Knapp School Libraries Project,
    37–38, 72, 165–66
Kodak, 73
Kodansha International, 73
Korean War, GI Bill for, 3
KRC Research and Consulting,
    35–36
Krettek, Germaine, 139
Krug, Judith F., 139, 150–51

Lancaster, F. Wilfred, 156, 170
Laura Bush Foundation, 40
Layton, Jeanne, 90
LC. *See* Library of Congress
learning: books/reading for, 47; competence in, 47; through distance, 44, 123; as lifelong, 18
Learning Today, 47
LeRoy Merritt Humanitarian Fund, 90, 150–51
"Let's Talk about It," 31
LexisNexis, 15, 168
Librarian of Congress, 49–50, 73
librarians: for academic libraries, 14, 42, 47, 48; ALA exchange for, 94; associations for, 2, 5, 81–87, *82, 83, 84,* 150; cataloging by, 13; challenges for, 154–55; collective bargaining/unionization for, 18, 19; demand *v.* supply for, 38; diversity among, 2, 5, 97–102, 151–52; education for, 5, 113; as electronic consultants, 44; ethnicity of, 2, 5, 97–102, 151–52; gender of, 2, 5, 18, 43, 95–97; influences upon, 2–3; interaction with, through Internet, 4, 10, 16, 17, 19, 21; international relations between, 5; journals for, 2, 8, 11, 39, 45, 47, 97, 105, 114, 115, 117, 126, 165, 169; leadership by, 154; listservs for, 16; NEH funding for, 31; online search training by, 15; reference instruction by, 17; reference service by, 4, 5, 10, 14–16, 17, 19, 21, 23, 145, 153–54, 167; salaries of, 86, 97; for school libraries, 37, 123; for special libraries, 52; stress/burnout of, 18; supply of, 4; training/certification of, 27, 31, 40, 86; women as, 2, 18, 43, 85, 96, 151–52, 168, 169
libraries: access to, 88, 153–54; acquisitions by, 7, *11,* 50; art reproductions in, 10; audio books in, 10, 30; automation of, 20, 21; blogging by, 21; buildings for, 4, 5, 23, 103–5, *104;* challenges for, 5; circulation statistics by, 4, 10, 34, *35;* Cold War and, 3; collection management by, 7; computers in, 2, 4, 19, 26, 44; cooperation among, 5, 12, 19, 21, 27, 31, 38–39, 43, 45–46, 59–65, 149–50; copiers in, 2; costs for, 26; digital collections for, 4, 10–11, 20, 22, 44, 107–8, 153–54; diversity within, 2, 5, 97–102, 151–52; electronic systems within, 7, 10, 30, 163; e-mail/WWW/listservs for, 16, 19, 21; equipment for, 2; federal funding for, 2, 5, 9, 25–26, 27, 31, 38, 42, 67–71, 149; filmstrips in, 10; fund-raising for, 18; future of, 5; GI Bill and, 3; golden age of, 4; Great Fear and, 3; growth of, 3–4, 23, 33, 36–37, 40–41, 47, 147–48; historical changes in, 2; as information gateway, 4, 5, 16–17; interior design of, 5, 104; I&R centers for, 14; management of, 5, 17–19; membership in, 14; multimedia kits in, 10; organization of, 18; outsourcing by, 19; personnel for, 14, 18, *19;* philanthrophy for, 5, 9, 25, 27, 71–76, 80; podcasting by, 21;

privatization of, 19; realia in, 10; reference service in, 4, 5, 10, 14–16, 17, 19, 21, 23, 145, 153–54, 167; resource sharing between, 19; responsibility for, 4; sculpture in, 10; segregation within, 24; slides in, 10; special collections within, 9; standardization among, 12, 151; status of, 155–59; strategic planning for, 18; in suburbia, 3, 24; taxation for, 4, 24, 25; technology for, 4, 5, 7, 10, 19–22, 30; types of, 5, 23–57, 156–58; for undergraduate, 14, 41; in urban setting, 3, 14, 24; usage of, 4; volunteers for, 76; weblog use by, 21. *See also* individual types of libraries

libraries, academic: Academic Facilities Act for, 42, 68, 165; ARL for, 41; Association of College and Research Libraries for, 42, 44; bibliographic instruction by, 14; buildings for, 103–5; collections of, 41, 44–46; computer labs within, 44; distance learning through, 44, 123; expenditures of, 41, 44, 45; *Faculty Status for Academic Libraries* (ACRL), 42; Farmington Plan for, 41, 164; federal funding for, 9, 42, 67–71, 149; growth of, 40–41, 147–48; *Guidelines for Two-year College and Learning Resources Program,* 41–42, 165; Higher Education Act for, 42, 68, 115, 124, 166; OPACS for, 43; problems for, 43; *Standards for College Libraries* for, 41, 44, 165; *Standards for Junior College Libraries,* 41–42, 165; *Standards for University Libraries* for, 43; Title III for, 42, 56, 60, 68, 149–50, 166

libraries, Carnegie, 9, 25, 27, 29, 72, 74–75, 80, 103, 164

Libraries of the Future (Licklider), 20, 166

libraries, presidential, 54–55, 68, 70, 147–48, 164

libraries, public: administration for, 26; *Adult Education Activities in Public Libraries* for, 30–31; adult services for, 30–32; audio books in, 10; automated circulation for, 26; budgets for, 24–25, 26; buildings for, 23, 103–5, *104*; children/young adult services by, 32–34, *34*; collection development of, 23, 29–30; *Cost Funding for Public Libraries* for, 28; demand *v.* supply of books for, 29–30; *Directions for Library Service to Young Adults* for, 33, 169; energy crisis and, 25; evaluation of, 27–28; expenditures index for, 26; federal funding for, 9, 25–26, 27, 67–71, 149; future of, 27–28; growth in, 23, 147–48; *Guidelines for Audiovisual Materials and Services for Public Libraries,* 27; homeless in, 24; immigration/migration and, 3, 24, 33; inflation and, 25; information highway access through, 26, 153–54; latchkey children in, 33; as literacy source, 31; *Minimum*

Standards for Public Library Systems, 27, 167; multimedia formats in, 10, 16, 17, 21, 26, 30, 163; *The National Plan for Public Library Service* (1948), 26–27, 97–98, 164; NCES data for, 34, *35*; *New Planning for Results* for, 29; *Output Measures for Public Libraries* for, 28, 170; *Output Measures for Public Library Services to Children: A Manual of Standardized Procedures* for, 29; outreach programs by, 31–32, 85; *Planning and Role Setting for Public Libraries* for, 28–29, 170; *Planning for Results: A Public Library Transformation Process* for, 29; *Planning Process for Public Libraries* for, 28, 169; *Post War Standards for Public Libraries,* 26; Public Library Association for, 86; Public Library Inquiry for, 27, 29, 72, 74–75, 164; *Public Library Mission Statement* for, 27–28, 169; *Public Library Plans for the Teen Age* for, 33; *Public Library Service: A Guide to Evaluation* for, 27, 165; readers' advisory/ guidance concepts by, 31; reading promotions by, 23, 30; reference service by, 4, 5, 10, 14–16, 17, 19, 21, 23, 145, 153–54, 167; resources for, 25; school/ community organizations and, 33; segregation within, 24; senior citizens and, 24; *Services and Resources for Children and Young Adults in Public Libraries* for, 34; services of, 23; social impact of, 24–25; Social Science Research Council study for, 27; standards for, 27, 151; *Standards for Children's Services in Public Libraries* for, 27, 166; *Standards for Work with Young Adults* for, 27, 165; story hours at, 32–33; as system members, 2, 23, 24; theft prevention by, 26, 166; Title III for, 42, 56, 60, 68, 149–50, 166; Vietnam War and, 25; weblogs by, 22; *Young Adult Services in the Public Library* for, 33

libraries, research: budgets for, 45; CLIR for, 76; Conspectus for, 45–46; cooperation between, 45–46, 149–50; journals for, 45; purchasing for, 46; RLIN for, 13, 43, 60, 70, 167, 168, 169; Title II-C for, 42

libraries, school: certified media specialist in, 40; closure of, 4; curriculum support by, 33, 123; government funding for, 9; growth of, 33, 36–37, 147–48; immigration/migration and, 33; *Information Power: Building Partnerships for Learning,* 39, 172; *Information Power: Guidelines for School Library Media Programs* for, 39, 170, 171; Laura Bush Foundation grants for, 40; library media specialist for, 37, 123, 155; media center for, 36–40; *Media Programs: District and School* for, 38, 169; NDEA for, 37; No Child Left Behind for, 39–40; private *v.* public, 40; public libraries and, 33; "Report of the Task Force on the Role of the School Library Media Programs in Networking" for, 38–39; *School Libraries for Today and Tomorrow: Functions and Standards* for, 37, 163; *Standards for School Library Programs* for, 37, 165; *Standards for School Media Programs* for, 38, 167; Title II for, 38; Title III for, 42, 56, 60, 68, 149–50, 166

libraries, special: activities of, 6; growth of, 50–51, 147–48; librarians for, 52; membership in, 52, *52*; publications for, 51, 166; Title III for, 42, 56, 60, 68, 149–50, 166; types of, 54, 156–58

Library-21 exhibit, 20, 85, 165. *See also* American Library Association

library and information science (LIS), 5, 6, 69, 82, 83, 84, 96–97, 113–25, *116, 117, 118,* 119, 126–27, 152–53, 156, 170, 171

Library and Information Science Research, 119

Library Awareness Program (FBI), 89

Library Bill of Rights (ALA), 87–88, 90, 98, 100, 150

Library Book Fellows Program (ALA), 170

library collections. *See* collections, library

Library College, 47

Library-College Journal. See Learning Today

Library Community Project (ALA), 31, 72

"Library Education and Manpower" (ALA), 115

Library Instruction Round Table (ALA), 47

Library Journal, 39, 97, 105, 115, 117, 169

Library Literature, 2, 31–32, 125

Library Literature Index (H.W. Wilson Co.), 170

library media centers. *See* libraries, school

Library of Congress (LC): automated national database by, 78; Carnegie Corporation grant for, 74–75; Cataloging in Publication by, 12, 168; Center for the Book in, 50, 155, 169; commemorative stamp for, 70; Digital Library Program for, 50, 73; expansion of, 49–50; Librarian of, 49–50, 73; MARC for, 12, 13–14, 21, 43, 60, 62, 78, 129, 148, 149, 158, 166; as national library, 49; *National Union Catalog of Pre-1956 Imprints* by, 12, 167, 170; NPAC for, 50; preservation by, 106, 107, 152, 168; on WWW, 50

Library Orientation Exchange (LOEX), 47

Library Power Project, 39

Library Research. See Library and Information Science Research

library service, hierarchy of, 27

Library Services Act (LSA), 25, 56, 67, 71, 165

Library Services and Construction Act (LSCA), 25, 42, 56, 60, 68, 149, 166, 171

Library Services and Technology Act (LSTA), 71, 171

Library Technology Project (LTP), 77
Library Technology Reports (CLR), 77, 126
Library Trends, 164
Library USA (ALA), 85, 114, 166
Licklider, J. C. R., 20, 166
Lindberg, Donald, 145
Lippincott Award, 129
LIS. *See* library and information science
listservs. *See* technology
Literacy Assembly (ALA), 86, 171
Literacy through School Libraries, 39–40
literature, library, 15, 125–27, *126*
lobbying, by professional associations, 38, 150
Lockheed Company, 15
LOEX. *See* Library Orientation Exchange
LSA. *See* Library Services Act
LSCA. *See* Library Services and Construction Act
LSTA. *See* Library Services and Technology Act
LTP. *See* Library Technology Project
Lubetzky, Seymour, 140
Lyman, Helen H., 30, 140

machine-readable catalog (MARC), 12, 13–14, 21, 43, 60, 62, 78, 129, 148, 149, 158, 166
MacLeish, Archibald, 49
Management Intern Program (CLR), 44
management, library, 5, 17–19
Management Review and Analysis Program (MRAP), 43–44

Mansell Publishers, 12
MARC. *See* machine-readable catalog
Margaret E. Monroe Award, 130
Margaret Mann Citation, 130
Marian Gould Gallagher Distinguished Service Award, 131
Marke, Julius, 145
Markey, Karen, 122
Martell, Charles, 156
Martin, Lowell, 140
Master's of Library Science (MLS), 1, 114–23, *116,* 126, 152, 164
Matheson, Nina W., 145
McCook, Kathleen de la Pena, 32, 140
McLuhan, Marshall, 7, 156, 165
Media Programs: District and School, 38, 169
Media Technical Assistants, 114–15
Medical Library Assistance Act (1965), 68
Medical Library Association Fellows, 131
Medicare, 3
MEDLARS, 78
MEDLINE system, 15, 168. *See also* National Library of Medicine
Mellon Foundation, 46
MEMEX machine, 15
Mersky, Roy, 145
microform, 9–10. *See also* technology
Microsoft Explorer, 4, 16, 19, 21, 163. *See also* Internet; technology
Middle East Librarians Association, 101
Middle States Commission on Higher Education, 48

Midwest InterLibrary Center
(MILC), 41, 59–60, 61, 164. *See also* Center for Research Libraries

migration. *See* immigration/ migration

MILC. *See* Center for Research Libraries; Midwest InterLibrary Center

Millen, Irene, 146

Miller Brewing Co., 73

Miller, Catherine K., 146

Miller, Philip L., 146

Minimum Standards for Public Library Systems (ALA), 27, 167

MIT Press, 20

MLS. *See* Master's of Library Science

Monteith Library Project, 47

Moon, Eric, 141

Morsch, Lucille, 131

Mosaic browser, 4, 16, 163. *See also* Internet; technology

MP3s. *See* technology

MRAP. *See* Management Review and Analysis Program

multimedia kits, 10

Mumford, L. Quincy, 12, 49–50

Music Library Association's Honorary Members, 131

Nader, Ralph, 70

National Advisory Commission on Libraries, 167

National Archives and Research Service, 54, 55

National Center for Educational Statistics (NCES), 11, 17, 30, 34, *34, 35,* 45, 48–49, 56

National Commission on Libraries, 69, 168

National Commission on Libraries and Information Science Act (1970) (NCLIS), 69, 153, 170

National Council for Teacher Accreditation (NCATE), 123

National Defense Education Act (NDEA), 37, 68

National Digital Newspaper Program, 110

National Endowment for the Arts, 166

National Endowment for the Humanities (NEH), 31, 107, 110, 166

National Foundation on the Arts and Humanities Act, 69

National Inventory of Library Needs (ALA), 116

National Legislative Day, 85, 168

National Library of Medicine (NLM), 15, 68, 78, 168

National Library Power Program (ALA), 171

National Library Week, 85, 153, 165

National Organization for Women (NOW), 3, 95–96, 162

The National Plan for Public Library Service (1948), 26–27, 97–98, 164

National Program for Acquisitions and Cataloging (NPAC), 50

The National Union Catalog of Manuscript Collections (CLR), 77

National Union Catalog of Pre-1956 Imprints, 12, 167, 170. *See also* cataloging; Library of Congress

Native Americans, library service and, 32, 101, 102, 152
NCATE. *See* National Council for Teacher Accreditation
NCES. *See* National Center for Educational Statistics
NCLIS. *See* National Commission on Libraries and Information Science Act
NDEA. *See* National Defense Education Act
NEH. *See* National Endowment for the Humanities
NELINET. *See* New England Information Network
NetLibrary. *See* Ohio College Library Center
Netscape Navigator, 4, 16, 163. *See also* computers; Internet; technology
networking, 5, 12, 13, 19, 21, 27, 31, 38–39, 43, 45–46, 59–65, 70, 74, 78, 149–50, 163, 167, 168, 169; P2P for, 163
New Directions in Library and Information Science Education (ALA), 121
New England Document Conservation Center, 106
New England Information Network (NELINET), 43, 78
New England Library Association, 106
New Planning for Results (ALA), 29
Newport Beach Public Library, 22
New Yorker, 108
New York Public Library (NYPL), 11, 26, 73, 172
New York Review of Books, 109
New York Times, 116

Nixon, Richard M., 4, 25, 55
NLM. *See* National Library of Medicine
No Child Left Behind, 39–40
NOW. *See* National Organization for Women
NPAC. *See* National Program for Acquisitions and Cataloging
NREN. *See* High Performance Computing Act
NSFNET, 170
NYPL. *See* New York Public Library

Oakley, Robert, 145
Objectives and Standards for Special Libraries (SLA), 51, 166
OCLC. *See* Ohio College Library Center
OCR. *See* Optical Character Recognition
Office for Diversity (ALA), 2, 5, 97–102, 151–52
Office for Intellectual Freedom (OIF), 89, 150–51, 167
Office for Library Education (ALA), 115
Ohio College Library Center (OCLC): alliances of, *61,* 61–62; CLR grant to, 78; establishment of, 21, 42–43, 61, 149, 167; FirstSearch by, 16; historical highlights of, 62–63; NetLibrary by, 10, 12–13, 169; PRISM by, 13, 171; WorldCat by, 8–9, *9,* 13, 62, 168. *See also* Online Computer Library Center, Inc.
OHIOLINK, 46
OIF. *See* Office for Intellectual Freedom

"100 of the Most Important Leaders We Had" *(American Libraries)*, 130

Online Computer Library Center, Inc. (OCLC), 57, 60, 61, 93, 149

online public access catalogs (OPACS), 4, 13, 15, 17, 19, 21, 26, 43, 153–54. *See also* technology

online resources, for digital collection, 4, 10–11, 22, 44, 107–8, 153–54

OPACS. *See* online public access catalogs

Optical Character Recognition (OCR), 110

ORBIT database, 15, 163

Output Measures for Public Libraries: A Manual of Standardized Procedures (ALA), 28, 170

Output Measures for Public Library Services to Children: A Manual of Standardized Procedures (ALA), 29

outreach programs, 31–32, 85

Owen, Elizabeth U., 145

Owens, Major R., 100

P2P network. *See* technology

paperbacks, 3

paraprofessionals, library, 18, *19*

Patriot Act, 91, 150

periodicals. *See* serials

personnel, library, 14, 18, *19*

philanthropy, to libraries, 9, 25, 27, 29, 71–76, 80, 103, 164. *See also* Carnegie Corporation

Phillips, 16

phonographs. *See* technology

Pizer, Irwin H., 145

Planning and Role Setting for Public Libraries (ALA), 28–29, 170

Planning for Results: A Public Library Transformation Process (ALA), 29

Planning Process for Public Libraries (ALA), 28, 169

podcasting. *See* technology

Polaroid Corporation, 73

Post War Standards for Public Libraries, 26

Powell, Lawrence Clark, 141

preservation, of library materials, 5, 55, 79, 105–11, 152, 168

Preservation Policy (ALA), 107

Presidential Libraries Act (1955), 54–55, 68, 70, 164

Presidential Library System, 54

Presidential Recordings and Materials Preservation Act, 55

President's Committee on Libraries, 167

PRISM, 13, 171. *See also* cataloging; Ohio College Library Center

publication, book, 2, 4, 7, 8, *8*, 46–47

Public Law 480, 68

Public Library Association, 86

Public Library Inquiry, 27, 29, 72, 74–75, 164

Public Library Mission Statement (ALA), 27–28, 169

Public Library Plans for the Teen Age (ALA), 33

Public Library Service: A Guide to Evaluation (ALA), 27, 165

racial discrimination, 86, 97–98, 100

Read About Me Project, 73

Readers' Advisory concept, 31

Reader's Guide to Periodical Literature (H.W. Wilson Co.), 170

reading, as a skill, 23, 30, 32, 154–55

Reagan, Ronald, 25, 50

realia, 10

reference service, 4, 5, 10, 14–16, 17, 19, 21, 23, 145, 153–54, 167

REFORMA: The National Association to Promote Library and Information Services to Latinos and the Spanish-Speaking, 100–101

"Report of the Task Force on the Role of the School Library Media Programs in Networking," 38–39

Research Libraries Group (RLG), 13, 43, 59, 60, 63–64, 168

Research Library Information Network (RLIN), 13, 43, 60, 70, 167, 168, 169

Research Strategies: A Journal of Library Concepts and Instruction, 47

Reuters, 73

Ristow, Walter, 141

RLG. *See* Research Libraries Group

RLG Conspectus, 45–46

RLIN. *See* Research Library Information Network

Rockefeller Foundation, 92

Rogers, Frank B., 145

"Role of Librarians in the Twenty-First Century" (Martell), 156

The Role of Women in Librarianship, 1876–1976: The Entry, Advancement and Struggle for Equalization in One Profession

(Heim; Weibel), 96, 169. *See also An Account of Sex: An Annotated Bibliography on the Status of Women in Librarianship*

Rollins, Charlemae, 141–42

Roosevelt, Franklin D., 54

RQ, 126, 165

R.R. Bowker LLC, 125–26, 156

Rules for Descriptive Cataloguing in the Library of Congress, 12, 164. *See also* cataloging

Sayers, Frances C., 142

Schiller, Anita, 96

Scholarly Publishing and Academic Resources Coalition (SPARC), 46, 93

School Libraries for Today and Tomorrow: Functions and Standards (ALA), 37, 163

School Library Journal, 39

School Library Manpower Project, 38

School Library Media Quarterly (AASL), 39

School Media Quarterly (AASL). *See School Library Media Quarterly*

sculpture, 10

segregation, within libraries, 24

Se-Lin labeling system, 77

senior citizens, public libraries and, 24

Senior Fellowship Program (CLR), 44

serials, 2, 8–9, *9,* 12

Services and Resources for Children and Young Adults in Public Libraries (NCES), 34

Shaw, Ralph R., 142

Shera, Jesse H., 114, 129, 142, 164
Shores, Louis, 47, 143
SLA. *See* Special Libraries
  Association
SLA Hall of Fame, 131
SLA Professional Award, 131
*Slow Fires: On the Preservation of
  the Human Record* (film), 79, 107
Social Responsibilities Round Table
  (ALA), 85, 168
Social Science Research Council
  (ALA), 27. *See also* American
  Library Association; Carnegie
  Corporation; standards, library
SOLINET, 43, 78
Sony Corporation, 16
Southern Association of Colleges
  and Schools, 48
South Huntington Library, 22
SPARC. *See* Scholarly Publishing
  and Academic Resources Coalition
The Speaker (ALA), 86, 100, 169
Special Libraries, 52
Special Libraries Association (SLA),
  51–54, 93, 100, 131
Special Libraries Association
  Honorary Members, 131
Spectrum Initiative (ALA), 102, 172
Stam, Deidre C., 110
Standard Book Number (ISBN), 12,
  13–14, 167
*Standards for Children's Services in
  Public Libraries* (ALA), 27, 166
Standards for College Libraries, 41,
  44, 165
*Standards for Community, Junior,
  and Technical College Learning
  Resource Programs,* 171
*Standards for Junior College
  Libraries,* 41–42, 165

*Standards for Library Functions at
  the State Level,* 56, 166
*Standards for School Library
  Programs* (AASL), 37, 165
*Standards for School Media
  Programs* (AASL/DAVI), 38, 167
*Standards for Services to the Blind
  and Visually Handicapped,* 167
Standards for University Libraries,
  43
*Standards for Work with Young
  Adults* (ALA), 27, 165
standards, library, 27, 29, 37, 38, 41,
  43, 44, 56, 151, 165, 166, 167
State and Regional Achievement
  Award, 90
*The State of Preservation Program
  in American College and
  Research Libraries: Building a
  Common Understanding and
  Action Agenda* (Kenney; Stam),
  110
St. Clair, Guy, 145
Steinbeck, John, 87
Stephens College, 47
Stone, Elizabeth W., 143
story hours, 32–33
Swell, Winfred, 145

Taft, 76
Tauber, Maurice, 143
taxation, for libraries, 4, 24, 25
technology: audiovisual materials as,
  9, 10, 16, 27, 30, 72, 74–75;
  automated circulation through,
  26; blogging as, 21; for
  communication, 4, 12, 16, 19, 21;
  copiers as, 2; database access
  through, 26, 153–54; desktop
  publishing as, 21; digital

collections as, 4, 10–11, 22, 44, 107–8, 153–54; during/after WWII, 3, 148; e-books as, 11, 153–54, 172; e-mail as, 16, 19, 21; facsimiles as, 21; film evolution as, 10, 26, 30; Google as, 11, 172; iPods as, 21, 22, 163; JSTOR digital backup files as, 46, 93; library instruction for, 46–48; listservs as, 16; microform as, 9–10; Microsoft Explorer as, 4, 16, 19, 21, 163; Mosaic as, 4, 16, 163; MP3s as, 22; Navigator as, 4, 16, 163; online catalogs as, 4, 13, 15, 17, 19, 21, 26, 43, 153–54; P2P as, 163; phonographs as, 10; podcasting as, 21, 22, 163; for printing, 8; television as, 3, 32, 108; theft prevention through, 26, 166; VCR as, 10; video/film as, 10, 26, 30; weblog as, 21; Webmaster, 44; WWW as, 4, 10, 16, 19, 21, 44, 48, 50, 148, 163

Telecommunication Act, 71, 171

television. *See* technology

theft, prevention of, 26, 166

Thomas, Lucille C., 143–44

Thomison, Dennis, 85–86

Thompson, James, 156, 170

Title II, 38

Title II-A/B/C, 38, 42, 68, 115, 124, 166

Title II-C, 42

Title III, Interlibrary Cooperation, 42, 56, 60, 68, 149–50, 166

Title IV, 68

"Toward a National Program for Library and Information Science" (NCLIS), 69

training, librarians', 31. *See also* certification, librarians'

Truman, Harry, 49, 54

Ulrich's Periodical Directory, 2, 8. *See also* serials

UNESCO, 92

unionization, for librarians, 18, 19

Union List of Serials (CLR), 77

United States Information Agency (USIA), 93, 170

University of Illinois Library Research Center, 26, 34, *35*

University of Michigan School of Information, 36

U.S. Census, 102

USIA. *See* United States Information Agency

U.S./Japan Conference on Library and Information Services in Higher Education, 92

U.S. Office of Education, 25, 115, 162

videocassette recorder/player (VCR). *See* technology

Vietnam War, libraries and, 25

"Vision ALA Goal 2000 — Intellectual Participation" (ALA), 171

Vocational Education Bill, 69

"Voices and Visions," 31

Vormelker, Rose, 145

Vosper, Robert G., 144

Wallace Foundation, 74

War on Poverty. *See* Great Society's War on Poverty

Washington Library Network (WLN), 43, 78

Watanabe, Ruth, 146
Wayne State University, 47
weblog. *See* technology
Webmaster. *See* technology
Wedgeworth, Robert, 85, 100, 144
Weibel, Kathleen, 96, 169
Western New York Library
    Resources Council (WNYLRC),
    64–65
Wheeler, Joseph, 131
White, Herbert, 145
White House Conference on
    Libraries, 69–70, 153, 169, 171
White House Conference on School
    Libraries, 40
William K. Kellogg Foundation, 74
Winfrey, Oprah, 32, 75
W. J. Barrow Laboratory, 79
W. K. Kellogg Foundation, 36, 122
WLN. *See* Washington Library
    Network
women: *An Account of Sex: An
    Annotated Bibliography on the
    Status of Women in
    Librarianship,* 96; ALA Task
    Force on the Status of Women,
    96, 168; ALA Task Force on

Women for, 85; *The Feminine
    Mystique* for, 3, 95, 162;
    feminism and, 3, 95–96, 162;
    NOW for, 3, 95–96, 162; pay
    equity for, 86, 97; *The Role of
    Women in Librarianship,
    1876–1976: The Entry,
    Advancement and Struggle for
    Equalization in One Profession,*
    96, 169; status of, as librarians,
    2, 18, 43, 85, 96, 151–52, 168,
    169; Women Library Workers, 96
WorldCat, 8–9, *9,* 13, 62. *See also*
    cataloging; Ohio College Library
    Center
World War II (WWII), 1, 2, 3, 148
World Wide Web (WWW), 4, 10,
    16, 19, 21, 44, 48, 50, 148, 163.
    See also Internet; technology
Wright, Louis B., 77, 144
WWII. *See* World War II
WWW. *See* World Wide Web

Young Adult Library Services
    Association (ALA), 74
*Young Adult Services in the Public
    Library* (ALA), 33

About the Author

George S. Bobinski is dean/professor emeritus at the State University at Buffalo, where he served as dean of the School of Information and Library Studies for almost thirty years. Previously, he worked as an administrator of academic and public libraries. He has had many monographs and articles published pertaining to library history, including the seminal *Carnegie Libraries: Their History and Impact on American Public Library Development* (ALA,1969).